SHANGHAI 1935

An American lady's account of
the city and its high-society

RUTH DAY

Introduced by Andrew Field

EARNSHAW
BOOKS

Shanghai: 1935

By Ruth Day

ISBN-13: 978-988-8552-61-0

This book has been reset in 12pt Book Antiqua. Spellings and punctuations are left as in the original edition.

HISTORY / Asia / China

EB127

Published by Earnshaw Books Ltd. (Hong Kong)

CONTENTS

Introduction   1

1. Arrival And Introduction To Shanghai   21
2. More Adventures And Encounters In Shanghai 43
3. Trip To Peiping/Peking   91
4. Last Days In Shanghai And Departure   107

About The Authors   137

NOTE

Some spelling inconsistencies in the original edition of this book have been corrected for this edition, but spellings are mostly left as they were originally published.

INTRODUCTION

BY ANDREW D. FIELD

In 1935, an American woman named Ruth Day traveled to Shanghai to spend time with her mother and step-father, who had been living in that city on the coast of China for six years. After reading her mother's letters for so many years, she also wanted to see the city and country firsthand. Her first and only visit, which also involved a brief trip to Peking (Beijing), lasted around six weeks between March and April 1935. After she returned to the United States, she published this book documenting her China trip and the people, places, and experiences she saw and had there. The book had a very limited print run of 200 copies, some of which eventually made their way into libraries, though one can safely assume that most copies were given as gifts to family and friends.

Sixty years later, in the mid-1990s, while I was

at Columbia University conducting research for a doctoral dissertation on the history of Shanghai and its infamous Jazz Age nightlife, I came across her book in the New York Public Library. I remember those days fondly, me shuffling through the large black index volumes of the NYPL searching for books that might provide unique insights into the city during its heyday in the 1920s and 1930s. I went through the indexes carefully, found titles of interest relating to Shanghai, ordered them at the counter, and waited for them to arrive so that I could pore through them while sitting at one of the tables in the cavernous main reading hall. I discovered many interesting books in the collections of the NYPL that shed light on the city's past, but this book in particular struck me as being remarkable because of Ruth Day's detailed and unvarnished descriptions of people, places, and experiences encountered during her trip. It was a window into a lost world. I made a copy of the entire book and kept it in my personal collection of research materials.

While researching the Jazz Age in Shanghai, I came across many lavish descriptions of the ballrooms and night clubs that operated in the city during its era as the "Paris of the East." Yet despite being a tourist who only attended a few of them once, Ruth Day's descriptions of establishments such as the Sky Terrace Ballroom of the Park Hotel, the Paramount Ballroom, the Del Monte, and the Majestic Café and Cabaret were among the most vivid, precise, and detailed that I encountered. Not only did she describe and list the people she met in those places and provide information on what they were doing, how they looked and danced, and what they wore, but she also took pains to describe the venues themselves with the eye of an architect or a designer. She also did the same for the numerous other places she visited during her trip, including people's private homes, as well as public theaters, restaurants, temples, and many other places.

Ruth Day's vivid descriptions of Shanghai nightlife, limited though they may be coming from the eye of a casual temporary visitor, made such an impression on me that I included them in the introductions to both of my books on Shanghai: my first book *Shanghai's Dancing World* and also *Shanghai Nightscapes*—the latter co-written with sociologist James Farrer. In the introduction to that book, James and I compare Ruth

Day's detailed account of her nights on the town in 1935 with one of our many nights in Shanghai in the 2000s. Other than these two books and some references to her work in pieces that I wrote and published on my website Shanghaisojourns.net, I can find no other references to her book online. Hopefully this will change as other readers discover her book and the treasures that lie within it.

Recently I shared my copy of Ruth Day's book with the publisher Graham Earnshaw. I had just collaborated with Graham on the republication of American jazz bandleader Whitey Smith's invaluable memoir of 1920s-1930s Shanghai, *I Didn't Make a Million*. Ruth Day certainly did not share the invaluable insider's view of Shanghai that Smith provides in his memoir—after all, she was just a tourist, while he was "the man who taught China to dance." Even so, I believe that her book also stands the test of time, providing a unique window into the lives, spaces, and experiences of the elite society of Shanghai just before it all came crashing down through the forces of war, invasion, occupation, and revolution.

When Graham decided to republish Ruth Day's book, he asked me to write a foreword to the publication. I immediately came to the realization that I knew next to nothing about her. Nor could I easily find any information about her online. So task at hand, I put on my historian's hat and went to work.

By reading her memoir more carefully and by searching online through various newspaper archives, I was able to piece together the story of her life and of her family. I also learned a great deal more about why her visit to Shanghai was such an interesting and fruitful one, as well as the main reason why her mother and step-father were living in the city during that era.

The more I learned, the more interested I became in their story, and came to understand more about why Ruth Day was able to produce such a valuable and unique snapshot of Old Shanghai during the height of its golden era. I combed through online newspaper archives including *The China Press*, *The Boston Globe*, and *The Springfield Republican*, as well as some other sources such as college alumni publications. Twenty years ago, when I first encountered her book, this kind of research would have been nearly impossible. Now, with the digitization of newspapers and other archives and their accessibility online, almost anything is possible, and I found myself working day and night, even while in bed, piecing together the story.

In 1892, Ruth Day was born into the world as Ruth Van Buren Hugo in Boston. Her parents were Jane Van Buren Hugo née Salisbury and George B. Hugo, who was possibly a descendant of the great French novelist Victor Hugo. Her father was in the liquor industry and he was also a prominent civic leader in Boston and eventually became President of the Massachusetts Employers Association. Her mother was an educated woman, who had graduated from DePauw University in 1890. She eventually became known for her skills in cultivating and designing rock gardens.

Ruth Van Buren Hugo was educated in Boston and attended Miss May's School, which was later consolidated into the independent school Brimmer and May in Chestnut Hill. In 1915, at the tender age of 23, she married Morgan Glover Day (1892-1975), a Harvard graduate of class of 1914 and a member of the prominent Day family of the city of Springfield in western Massachusetts. For the next thirty-five years, she lived with her husband in Springfield, in a residence on Mulberry Street. Boston and Springfield society knew her as Mrs. Morgan Day according to the convention of the age, and that is how she was known in all the newspapers.

Together they raised two sons, Robert Wolcott Day (1917-2011), and George Van Buren Day (1921-2011). There is very little information in the newspapers on Morgan Day, but one interesting tidbit is that he and Mrs. Morgan Day co-wrote skits and historical plays that were performed on the radio. Mrs. Morgan Day received far more press coverage than her husband. She became known in Springfield as a community leader and a member of the Junior League and also as a talented thespian. She appears in *The Springfield Republican* on many occasions, mostly having to do with her roles in various plays that were being staged.

For example, in the Junior League's 1930 staging of the children's play "Snow White and the Seven Dwarfs," she performed the role of Queen Brangomar. She also performed in many other plays in the 1920s and 1930s, usually in supporting roles. She was also involved in many other civic activities and organizations. At the same time, she was undoubtedly busy raising her two young sons.

In 1925, Ruth Day's father George B. Hugo died in

the city of Springfield. Within two years, her mother Jane Van Buren Hugo was remarried to an old college friend, Dr. Frederick Albert Cleveland, who had also graduated from DePauw University in 1890. Dr. Cleveland had also lost his first wife Jessica England Cleveland in 1926 (they were married in 1902, and they had raised a son named Lindsay). Thus, her mother became known as Mrs. Frederick A. Cleveland.

Dr. Frederick A. Cleveland (1865-1946) was by far the most prominent member of Ruth Day's family. After graduating from DePauw in 1890, and working for a few years as a lawyer, he went on to earn a Ph.D. in finance at the University of Pennsylvania in 1900. He became known as an advocate of budget reforms and an expert on municipal budgets and accounting. In the early 1900s, while serving as a Professor at New York University, he conducted important work on behalf of Mayor McLellan of New York City to reorganize the city's financial administration and accounting practices. According to his obituary published in the *Boston Globe* on January 28, 1946, he helped to expose the "shady dealings of New York borough heads" and was "at loggerheads" with the bosses of the ill-famed Tammany Hall.

Dr. Cleveland's work in New York City earned him the recognition of the federal government. In the 1910s, he worked under the Taft Administration and was Chairman of the Commission on Economy and Efficiency from 1911-1913. He also worked in the areas of Indian Affairs and for the Customs Service of New York. It seems that his skills in organizing financial accounting and administration were in great need in this era of progressivism, particularly when it came to "cleaning up" the corrupt modern city.

In 1919, Dr. Cleveland joined the faculty of Boston University as the new Chair of United States Citizenship. He spent the next ten years at the university and took up residence in Norwood. Meanwhile, he published a significant number of books and articles on a wide range of topics including budgeting, banking, finance, government funds, administration, citizenship, constitutional government, and democracy, covering an equally wide range of institutions from the U.S., French, and Canadian governments, to cities, to the railroads.

In 1929, Dr. Cleveland accepted a request to join a commission of American experts to travel to China to assist the new Chinese national government with stabilizing its finances. The head of the commission was Dr. Edwin W. Kemmerer, a professor at Princeton University. This was indeed a Herculean task, given the complexity of China's governance and its finances; although Dr. Cleveland expected to be in China for only a few months, he ended up staying for six years along with his second wife, Jane.

In 1931, Dr. Cleveland accepted a request from T. V. Soong (Song Ziwen), Finance Minister of the Chinese national government and brother-in-law of national leader Chiang Kai-shek, to take an executive position in the Finance Ministry as the acting associate chief administrator of the salt gabelle. This was the first time that an American had been given an executive appointment in the Chinese national government and he was in charge of a very important stream of national government revenue, amounting to 85 million U.S. dollars annually. Under the astute leadership of Dr. Cleveland, who had headed the accounting and now was in charge of the collecting operation of salt revenue as well, he was able to help increase collections to over $160 million by 1933.

In September 1931, the Japanese Army provoked an invasion of Manchuria. Soon afterwards, Dr.

Cleveland reported that the Japanese army had seized 2.6 million U.S. dollars of salt revenues from the Bank of China and Bank of Communications in Changchun. The report made its way to the League of Nations and stirred up a great deal of protest. It was reported in the *Boston Globe* and other U.S. newspapers at the time, and Dr. Cleveland gained even further prominence nationally.

I could go on describing in even greater detail the work that Dr. Cleveland did on behalf of the Chinese government, as well as his continual frustrations in dealing with the level of corruption he encountered along the way, but that is the subject of another paper. As it relates to our topic of the book that his step-daughter Ruth Day wrote, the significance of Dr. Cleveland's work in China is that while Mrs. Morgan Day did not write specifically about the work of her step-father except in very general descriptive terms, the story of her China trip reflects the high position and the deep respect in which her step-father and mother were held in Shanghai and in Chinese elite society.

While reading her book, one encounters many of the movers and shakers of modern Chinese history.

One episode she describes in great detail is a visit to the home of Lord and Lady Li Ching-mai (Jingmai) on Avenue Haig (now Huashan Road). I had wondered, reading the book, what connection her family had that would result in an invitation to one of the most prominent families of modern China. After all, this was the family home of the great patriarch, general, and patriot of the Qing Dynasty, Li Hongzhang. When one considers Dr. Cleveland's role in the Chinese government, it becomes readily apparent why Ruth Day and her parents were on the lofty list, which was published in full in *The China Press*. It reads like a *Who's Who* of Shanghai, and includes luminaries such as Sir Victor Sassoon, Dr. and Madame Wellington Koo, Mr. H. E. Morriss, as well as many other leaders of Shanghai's business, government, and civic society. Not only does Mrs. Morgan Day take pains to describe the party and all of the people she encountered there, she also provides detailed descriptions of the home itself as well as the gardens, which are still there today.

Another event here worth noting is a cocktail party that her mother and step-father arranged for her soon after her arrival in Shanghai. It was held in the Sky Terrace ballroom on the fourteenth floor of the Park

Hotel, which one can also still visit today. Once again, the guest list published in *The China Press* reads like a Who's Who listing of some of the prominent figures in the city including the Shanghai Mayor Wu Te-chen (Tiecheng), as well as the Japanese Minister Akira Ariyoshi, Italian Ambassador V. Lojacono, U.S. Consul General Edwin S. Cunningham, Sir Frederick and Lady Maze, and dozens of other guests representing the city's business, government and civic leadership.

At the end of her China trip, Ruth returned to the United States with a long journey by passenger liner that took her via Japan, to resume her duties as a mother, wife, and civil society leader in Springfield. One imagines that she went back to her normal life while taking some time to compile her notes and write this manuscript. Given the amount of detail that went into the book, one can assume that she was assiduous at note-taking during her trip, with the idea that she would publish her experiences somehow upon her return. Or perhaps somebody had suggested at the very beginning that she write a book about her journey. She may have also saved newspaper clippings from *The China Press* which featured many articles about her while she was visiting Shanghai in March and

April 1935.

The book was apparently published later the following year, in 1936. I was only able to find two book reviews of *Shanghai 1935* upon its publication. One was published in the *Los Angeles Times* on January 24, 1937 with the reviewer calling the book a "pleasantly informative account of the writer's experiences in China, chatty, casual and without any show of authority." The reviewer also noted that Ruth was "a keen observer, curious about all phases of oriental life." The other review appeared in the *Springfield Republican* on December 20, 1936. Its writer observed that "Shanghai" lived up to its explicit title and gives a personal impression of Chinese culture, moods and personalities as they were observed by an American traveler. "The author makes it evident that she is attempting no treatise on the Chinese, and advancing no argument for or against the national mode of life or convictions. Privileged to enter the homes of the city's personages, and meeting them on a plane of friendliness and intellectual appreciation, she has written an informal but animated description of their domestic and social activities." The review also noted that the book provides "accounts of odd customs observed with ceremonial precision by household heads," and that all of her experiences were written out with a mixture of "humor and frankness."

Perhaps because of her relatively low status as a woman (Mrs. Morgan Day, never Ruth Day in the newspapers) and her lack of academic credentials, her book was not taken seriously in its day, and it disappeared into obscurity. Fortunately, somebody was perspicacious enough to place a copy in the New York Public Library where a budding historian would one day find it, recognize the treasures hidden inside, and bring it back for a second life with the help of a publisher who specializes in resuscitating such manuscripts.

As for Mrs. Morgan Day, she sank back into obscurity herself, appearing only a few more times in the papers over the following years. It is not clear whether she made any attempt to give talks about her experiences in China or about her book—perhaps she felt that she lacked the authority to do so. On the other hand, her mother did give some public presentations based on her six years of living in China and published at least one newspaper article about China.

In 1939, Morgan and Mrs. Morgan Day's first

son Robert Wolcott Day was married to Joan Stuart Thompson. Their second son George married much later in 1952 to Katharine Miser. Both sons went on to pursue successful careers. Robert worked in advertising, and George became an expert and leader in the aluminum industry. Both sons had families of their own.

It is also unclear what happened to the Clevelands. One obituary for Dr. Cleveland published after his death in 1946 states that he and Mrs. Cleveland separated after their return to Boston in 1936. Dr. Cleveland returned to his position at Boston University and retired in 1939. He continued to perform civic duties in his town of Norwood, being involved in the School Committee and helping to oversee the construction of new schools. Today, a school in Norwood, the F. A. Cleveland Elementary School, bears his name. In 1937, Dr. Cleveland was awarded the Emblem of the Order of Blue Jade by the Chinese government. Ruth Day must have gone to live with her mother or vice versa after her sons had married. In any case, she and her mother Jane resided at 3611 Henry Hudson Parkway in Riverdale, New York for the remainder of their lives. Morgan apparently went to live with or near his son Robert, for he died in Los Angeles in 1975, and was buried in his hometown of Springfield. Jane Van Buren Salisbury Hugo Cleveland died in 1956 at the age of 89, and Ruth Van Buren Hugo Day passed away in 1964 at the age of 71.

Andrew D. Field
Shanghai, 2019

SHANGHAI 1935

RUTH DAY

THE SAUNDERS STUDIO PRESS
CLAREMONT CALIFORNIA 1936

This first edition, printed on Worthy Brochure Wove,
is limited to 200 copies.

1

Arrival And Introduction To Shanghai

I WAKED suddenly, feeling that something strange and exciting was going to happen. Daylight was coming through the porthole, and I thought the ship must have stopped, there was so little motion. The only sounds were the swish-swish of wet mops drawn across the decks, and the occasional pad-pad of a Chinese "boy" in the corridor. And then I remembered, we were due to arrive in Shanghai that afternoon. I jumped out of bed and rushed to the porthole. It was early dawn, and the sun was rising through a yellow haze, a haze that merged into the yellow muddy sea. I looked out of the porthole for a long time, trying to realize that the distant hazy shore was really China.

The S. S, Hoover was due to dock at Shanghai at two in the afternoon, yet at noon there were only thatched mud huts scattered along the muddy banks of the river, and nothing that remotely resembled a city, in sight. At this point the Whang-poo River is very crooked and narrow, and I wondered whether the Hoover could possibly navigate without running aground. At any moment around one of the many curves I expected to see Shanghai, but not until five o'clock in the afternoon did I see any indication of a city. Some tall buildings were visible in the distance through the yellow haze, and literally hundreds of all kinds of queer Chinese craft crowded the river.

Just as it was growing dark a small tender put out from an electric-lighted dock, and on the top deck, I discovered my mother, whom I had not seen for six years. I rushed to the lower deck with my passport and papers in an effort to be the first to leave the ship. I then received my first lesson in the ways of the Chinese. Speed, in either social intercourse or business, is one of the very few good qualities that they have not. On the lower deck, the Chinese port officials had just come aboard. They smiled genially and leisurely walked to their seats at a small table. Taking their time they finally settled themselves and drew out their pencils, rather bewildered by the crowds of passengers who were surging about in great disorder. All this confusion was in striking contrast to my experience two days earlier at Yokohoma, Japan, where attention to order and detail were carried beyond all reason. I must say that I prefer the Chinese way nevertheless, in spite of the confusion.

At the dock we were met by the Chinese chauffeur in a Buick limousine. I was disappointed! I had imagined myself riding in rickshas while visiting China, for I made the mistake usual among foreigners, of thinking of rickshas as native conveyances for the Chinese, when in reality they were introduced originally, solely for the pleasure of the foreigner! *

Quotation from Chinese Testament, S. Tretiakov.

"In China, these little carriages are called yang-che (rickshas) which means foreign carriage. They were introduced into China about thirty years ago and today provide a living for nearly a hundred thousand coolies. They are found mostly in the cites situated on the seashore or on level ground."

"This," said mother, "is the famous Bund of

Shanghai," as we emerged into an electric-lighted wide thoroughfare, swarming with rickshas, pedestrians and automobiles with all their horns blowing at once. We turned up Nanking Road, and I could well believe what I had been told about the Chinese people loving the brilliance of electric lights. I could almost believe that I was going up Broadway, for the street was literally a blaze of electric lights. But the effect was even more dazzling with the red and gold cloth business signs, hanging out like flags. The car sped up Nanking Road with the horn blowing constantly, to scare off the ricksha coolies who dashed out like chickens, utterly oblivious of traffic, of traffic lights or police. Finally we turned on to Bubbling Well Road and saw the fifteen story high Park Hotel towering above the other buildings.

I should have thought I was entering the Ritz-Carlton Hotel in Boston except for the Chinese people working there. My room was on the twelfth floor, overlooking the whole electric-lighted panorama of the business section of the International Settlement. A sign in letters three feet high, a few blocks away, read "Lion Beer." I just could not believe that I was really in China! I remember going to sleep that first night, thoroughly disillusioned, with all my romantic ideas about China, shattered by the sounds of street cars, the constant honking of automobile horns and the brilliant electric-lighted stores and theatres on Nanking Road. I was told later that six years ago there were hardly any electric lights, when my mother went out to Shanghai.

As I opened the window I heard the chattering ricksha coolies on the sidewalk twelve stories below. Some people on the lower floors of the hotel complained of being kept awake by their chatter, but to me the sound of their voices was like music, music that revived the lureful, mysterious China of my imagination. But it was night and I could not see how they looked. Later when I realized their really pitiful condition the sound of their voices would have depressed me. They sleep on the roadside between the shafts of their rickshas, at any time of day or night just like dogs. I was told that they, as well as all Chinese of the laboring classes, are run by Guilds, organized so that the head men make exorbitant profits. A ricksha coolie has to pay eighty cents, Chinese money, per day to the Guild for the privilege of dragging a ricksha. The average fare paid is twenty cents, Chinese money, for a mile, and many days the coolies can get no fares, as the supply, now with automobiles for taxi service, is greater than the demand. So with all their labor they are always in debt to the Guilds for their accumulated overdue fees and barely earn enough for a little rice to keep from starving. I have never seen a group of people who could so perfectly fit the term "the underdogs." The Sikh police, reminders of the British yoke, seem to take an especial joy in cuffing them about, and beating them with clubs. How I hated the arrogant attitude of those Sikhs! But I was told by an Englishman that my resentment was unreasonable, because the coolies would probably be killed by the motor traffic if it were not for the protection of the Sikhs. A typical British attitude! He then naïvely told me that the Sikhs were a fine lot of men, very shrewd in business, several of them having amassed large fortunes by the careful investment of their money acquired doing their duty in China. My sympathies were all with the Chinese, and a few days later I made up my mind to go walking all by myself among them and see them near to.

I left the hotel early in the afternoon and went down Nanking Road, considered the center of the most cosmopolitan business life in Shanghai. Imagine

Times Square with everyone dressed in Chinese clothes, running for street cars, dodging across streets between rickshas and motor busses, marked with Chinese characters along the sides; and chattering in high pitched, sing-song voices. Above all this din, imagine radios at every block, broadcasting Chinese music that sounds like cats howling, a constant repetitious refrain; open food shops with roasted chickens, looking as if they were varnished a dark brown and hanging in rows on hooks across the front of the shop overhead, and below on the counters all sorts of mushy-looking white cakes like dumplings not yet cooked for a stew, and big barrel-like steaming tins of gravy and meat, exposed to the dust of the street and whatever else! It seemed as if every other person was hawking and spitting, and after walking a few blocks, every time I heard a hawk I'd jump as if it were an automobile horn. If you can imagine all this, you will visualize a bit of this world-famous street. The shops were a strange mixture of the old and the new. Next to a native food shop might be an electric-lighted radio store, or a Chinese-owned department store. In one of these was displayed modernistic bedroom furniture, with the bed all made up, and the

figure of a black-haired lady lying on it. I was told that
the Chinese from the country had to be shown how a
bed was used, hence the reclining figure. One of the
fascinations of this street was to see the different types
of Chinese attracted to it. Some were plainly from
the country and wore round caps like the Russian
peasants, but they did not look like Russians because,
like most Chinese they had no hair on their faces.
They gazed in the shop windows with a look of dazed
wonder, and I felt a sort of kinship, knowing that I
too must appear just as wondering and just as odd.
That sense of being the only one of a kind, creates a
psychology of isolation, hard to understand unless
experienced. But I had very little time to think about
myself for I was so intrigued by the variety of sights
about me. I saw a young Chinese father, dressed in
the usual street clothes for men, the long drab-colored
coat and black satin cap, leading his little boy by the
hand and pointing out the sights of the city. At every
block, vendors of shoe laces with the laces hung over
a stick at full length, shouting, "velly pletty! Missy
buy?"

All kinds of things were sold along the street by
vendors carrying their wares in baskets at either end

of a bamboo pole balanced across their shoulders. They had live geese sitting sedately on flat baskets, looking very comical with their heads bobbing up and down at each loping amble of the carrier. I wondered why the geese did not fall off, and was told that their feet were wired to the bottom of the baskets. Potted flowering plants were carried this way also, making bright spots of color among drab clothing of the pedestrians.

There were ricksha boys everywhere, insisting that I ride. I always waived them away wistfully, because I had been advised not to ride in rickshas when I was alone. One of these boys was very provoked when I refused and followed me, dragging his ricksha with one hand and gesticulating with the other, while grumbling in a disgusted voice, "Walkee, walkee, walkee!" until one of my hated Sikhs beat him off.

I walked to the end of Nanking Road, to the Cathay Hotel, at the corner of the Bund and back to the Park Hotel, situated just beyond the intersection of Nanking and Bubbling Well Roads, a distance of about a mile, a thrilling mile by both day and night. It was always a maze of traffic. Buicks, Fords and Chevrolets were everywhere, and once I saw one lone antiquated Rolls Royce! Bicycles and rickshas wove a perilous course between automobiles, electric busses and street cars. It was surprising that the ricksha passengers especially were not annihilated, although they appeared quite unconcerned. One portly Chinese attracted my attention, for he completely filled in the width of the ricksha, bulging forward accordingly. He was leaning back with his black satin skull cap tipped well down on his forehead, smoking a very long black cigar that slanted upward at a most arrogant tilt. He looked as if he felt he were king of the world, quite disdainful of the tooting horns of the passing autos. These predominantly tooted the "How dry I am" strain, just then a novelty I was told. I felt there was no point in having those horns in Shanghai where liquid refreshment was plentiful, and where there was even a street named "Bubbling Well Road." I had asked about that name and was told that there really was a bubbling well at the other end of the road. The Chinese believe that a spirit keeps the well bubbling, and although it was in the centre of a main thoroughfare, a stone wall was built around it for protection, and a temple is at the side of the street where offerings may be purchased, to be thrown in to the well to insure the continuous bubbling. I was told that this temple was one of the richest in Shanghai from the sale of these offerings. There are street car tracks at either side of the walled-in well, and wide asphalt pavements swarming with vehicles of the machine age. Just another example of the survival of old superstitions amid modern improvements that makes Shanghai so fascinating!

One evening I had another walk on Nanking Road after ten o'clock at night, but not alone. I had told a friend of my mother's, that I should like to go out some night and see the street I had heard about, where certain kinds of Chinese girls could be seen soliciting although accompanied by their attendant Amahs, older women or mothers. The gentleman who invited me to go had lived in China for over thirty years and knew all the customs. He said we would have to walk if we wanted to see anything, so we started off from the Park Hotel, and walked about a quarter of a mile to the Chinese district off Thibet Road. I wanted adventure but I certainly was scared when we went into the side streets of that district! There was not a foreigner in sight and the streets were only lit by the single lights at each low doorway. I thought of the stories I had been told about kidnappers and thieves guilds, and that people of prominence had to pay the heads of these guilds not to molest them. I certainly hoped the proper persons had been paid, if by any chance I could be considered a person of prominence! Mother had told me about a sensational kidnapping and murder of a wealthy Chinese that she had seen from her window, when she was living at the Hotel Tiny in the French Concession. This Chinese gentleman's estate was next to the hotel, and evidently he had not paid enough to the kidnapper's guild! All these stories raced through my mind as we wandered through dark alleys for what seemed to me an eternal length of time. I felt as if there were sinister figures lurking in all the dark doorways, and was very glad that my companion looked so tall and strong! Suddenly in the darkness ahead of us, we heard a tinkling bell that sounded very alarming to me in my excited state, but in reality was no more mysterious than an ordinary cowbell. Out of the darkness as the sound came near there appeared a forlorn little boy leading a blind man, and ringing the bell, the usual way of protecting blind people. We passed through myriads of dark alleys without seeing a single girl;

we emerged on to brilliantly lighted Nanking Road. My courage returned with the lights, and when we saw a crowd gathering, way down another dark side street, we dashed down to see the excitement. We then discovered why we had seen no girls and Amahs for the police had picked that particular night to stage a "clean up". I was disappointed for I had been told that these girls are among the most beautiful to be seen anywhere in Shanghai! And I never did have a chance to see them later.

About a week after my arrival a party was given for me by my family at the Park Hotel in a ball room on the fourteenth floor. It was an afternoon reception and was a brainstorm for me. I had been given a list of names to study beforehand, but by the time I had shaken hands with a dozen people, my mind was a blank. Chinese names are so hard to remember. I told one Chinese lady how difficult it was for me, and she was much amused or else very polite, because she said that foreign names were almost impossible for her to recall also. There were about sixty Chinese people among the two hundred who came, among them Lord and Lady Li-Ching-Mei and their son and his wife (Lord Li-Hung-Chang of international fame).

Mayor Wu-Te-Chen (the famous mayor of Shanghai, who is responsible for the building of the modern city in the Kiang Wan district) and his wife. In the January 1935 issue of FORTUNE there are pictures of him and the development; Dr. Herman Liu, President of Shanghai College, and Mrs. Liu, who is the leader of many philanthropies among the Chinese women. There are about thirty Americans, from the Consulate and in various government positions, and many English people, among them Sir Frederick and Lady Maze. He is foreign head of the Chinese customs as Dr. Cleveland, my mother's husband was then foreign head of the Chinese Salt Revenue. Other English people were Sir John Brennan, head of the British consular service, and Lady Brennan; Sir Elly Kadoorie, the owner of the house popularly called the "marble hall" and one of the wealthiest men in Shanghai, I was told; Mr. Edwin Hayward, editor-in-chief of the NORTH CHINA DAILY NEWS, the leading British newspaper in Shanghai, thin, nervous and interesting, who insisted I heard later, but one cannot believe all one hears in Shanghai, that I must give the paper an interview, because he thought I must be a movie actress travelling incognito; the consuls and their wives from

Czechoslavakia, Sweden, The Netherlands, Germany, Austria, Po-land, Portugal, Belgium, France and Switzerland; the Italian Ambassador was the first from that country to represent Mussolini in China; the Japanese minister Ariyoshi and Mrs. Ariyoshi, and several other members of the Japanese diplomatic service and their wives were with them. Some of the latter wore foreign clothes and spoke English, while others wore Japanese clothes and spoke French. I remember I was quite pleased with myself because my indifferent French was understood. But both Japanese and Chinese ladies are very polite, having a reserved manner, a set smile. They always look as if they understood you but in return say very little. Later, at a Chinese dinner, I talked for several minutes to a sweet little Chinese Lady, who smiled and kept murmuring gently, "Poodung," as she sipped her tea. I thought that "Poodung" with tea meant something like "Cheerio" with cocktails. I told my mother about it later, and she was much amused, because "Poodung" means "I do not understand you." At the reception I was worried about subjects for conversation with the Chinese guests, but I was advised, if I could think of nothing else to say, to inquire about the children, and hope that there were some! Many of the Chinese ladies looked very young and it was difficult to guess who were mothers. They were dressed in modern style Chinese dresses, short sleeves, high collar and slit skirt, and smoked cigarettes, a special brand, "different from the foreign ladies!"

As the last guests left, I looked around that really lovely room. The walls and ceilings as well as the red pillars which surrounded the circular dance floor in the centre of the room were Chinese red with gold scroll-like designs. Two sides were glass windows which overlooked the electric-lighted panorama of foreign Shanghai in great contrast to the vast area of native Shanghai, shadowy and sinister in the twilight. And still it was hard for me to realize that I was actually in Shanghai, and had just met many of the people most vital to the making of history in the Far East. I was full of questions, for I had heard many wild rumors about them. But an American lady told me that the real truth was even more fantastic than the rumors, and I believe her now. I was in a whirl of excitement, learning all the gossipy details about the international group, as well as many interesting facts about the Chinese people. At a dinner given by an

American Advisor of the Chinese Finance Ministry, I met an American who was the president of the largest electrical company in Shanghai. He told me about the building of radios and broadcasting stations in China, and said that answers had been received from as far in the interior as Thibet, and that in some small places, where the majority of people cannot read or write, the radio was the only means of spreading news. He pointed out what a great help this would be in unifying the Chinese language. How strange it would be if an invention as modern as the radio should be a means of unifying a language as old as the Chinese! It might well be, for I had been told that the Chinese are very curious, which would make them anxious to know what was being said over the radio. Chinese curiosity was further illustrated by a story my mother told me about an experience she had, while on a picnic in the country. There were some Chinese women near the spot selected for the picnic, and as mother spread out the cloth and laid out the food, they gathered around, looking her all over and touching her clothes. As she bent over, she happened to look over her shoulder and was shocked to find that her skirt was held way up in the back and the women behind her were examining

her underpinnings with solemn interest. My mother is
a modest person and this episode was a great shock to
her, but she could not help seeing the funny side of it.
But these women after all were no more curious about
mother's clothes than I was about Chinese clothes for
I was interested, to say the least, to see the sleeves of
some long woolen underwear appearing under the
wide cuffs of a most beautiful coat of heavy Chinese
brocade worn by a Chinese gentleman, and from that
day always wondered what else they wore under their
beautiful silk robes. But I understood the reason for
the woolen underwear after going to a few Chinese
houses in evening clothes. They have no central
heating, and I hoped that the Chinese ladies were
equally well protected although my curiosity never
gave me enough courage to inquire or investigate!

I was constantly interested by the many kinds of
Chinese women whom I had the good fortune to
meet. At the Banker's Club on Peking Road at a tiffin,
that is a luncheon, I met several. The tiffin was given
by a Chinese lady, whose husband is the President
of a leading college in Shanghai. It was a Chinese
luncheon, served "Chinese way," on a large round
table with no cloth, and with the food set in the centre

in large dishes, all helping themselves with their own chopsticks, using the damp warm, turkish towelling face cloths that were passed, between courses instead of napkins. The conversation was most interesting, as several of the ladies were leaders in various progressive endeavors. One of them was especially interested in philanthropy and was the moving power in the establishment of a home for beggars in the new Chinese Civic Centre, in the Kiangwan district of Shanghai. She told about the need and destitution among the beggars, and of the cooperation among the enlightened Chinese women aiding her in the work. I was sorry I never managed to go out there to see the Home, but certainly saw enough of the beggars to know that her attempt was courageous, but the task is almost hopeless. At the traffic lights and along the streets the beggars literally swarm, old women, cripples, children and men. The latter exhibit terrible and revolting scars to enlist your sympathy. I was told that they deliberately scrape their legs and wrists raw, in a desperate effort to receive more alms. The children, I must confess, looked very healthy but frightfully dirty, and had not the technique of begging very well developed. Invariably they would grin broadly, while saying in a sing-song voice that had no pleading in it, "Nickle—dime—penny please!" or "No Mammy—no chow—penny please!"

Another lady at the tiffin, pretty as a picture in her lavender Chinese dress, was the director of the birth control activities in Shanghai. She said that the good accomplished so far, was not as much as she hoped, because the Kuomintang, although originally supporting the idea of birth control propaganda, as a means of alleviating the sufferings among the poor, was now against it, feeling like Mussolini, that numbers were necessary for race supremacy. After seeing the swarms of people everywhere, I felt that China should be the nation supreme at the present date if only numbers were necessary. Later on while talking to the son of one of the most eminent statesman, a Chinese of the Manchu Dynasty, and who therefore believes in the ancient marriage customs, explained a fact relevant to this discussion. He said that if a wife bore a child, neither he nor his relatives if he died could ever put her aside. She would always receive the homage of a No. 1 wife. He might have any number of concubines and their children, but they would hold no position of honor in the family. I realized then the difficulties of trying to popularize birth control, when having a child could mean so much in material wealth and honor to a wife, although it might appeal to the concubines.

I was ever so impressed by the modern views of this group of cultured Chinese women. They told me about the many activities of the Chinese women of today, among them being, the ownership and administration of a bank with no men employees or advisers. I later told my friend of thirty years experience in China about my admiration and surprise, especially about their interest in philanthropy, and he very cynically remarked, that it had become quite the fashion among the foreign educated Chinese women to be philanthropic, and warned me to be sure to compliment them all equally, as there was a lot of jealousy among them. Another typically British attitude! I remember telling him that that kind of jealousy was not confined to Chinese women, or to women alone either. The more Chinese people I met, the more certain I became, that human nature is quite the same everywhere, despite nationalities or religions, and Shanghai society offered potent proof of this fact, with the many nationalities represented.

2

MORE ADVENTURES AND ENCOUNTERS IN SHANGHAI

ONE EVENING, we went to a musicale at the house of the Italian Ambassador, Count Lojacono, in the French Concession. He was the first Ambassador sent by Mussolini to China, and strangely enough resembled him in appearance. His wife was a charming Italian woman in her late forties, who did not speak English, but greeted her guests in French. They were assisted by two young attaches, one the secretary of the Embassy, the Marquis di Cettadini Cessi, who had the reputation of being very popular with the ladies, and I do not blame the ladies, and the other young man, Count Bonarelli, Counsellor to the Embassy.

The house was late Victorian, and the musicale took place in a central room, a continuation of the hallway. A large circular bay window was at one side and a large fireplace with a stone mantel reaching to the high ceiling at the opposite side. The dark oak wainscotting also reaching to the ceiling made a lovely background for the draperies of a Chinese yellow, money pattern gauze silk. The servants flitting about in their long white coats, with short scarlet sleeveless silk jackets, the usual costume for Chinese servants, with colors of the over jackets different in different houses, lent an oriental atmosphere. I wore a black velvet dress and sat on the circular settee, under the yellow curtained bay windows with the wife of the French Consul, a red haired, highly rouged lady, at my right, and the wife of the German Consul, a sweet faced lady with pale blonde straight hair parted in the middle, at my left. Neither could speak English, so I was put to it, speaking French to my right and German to my left.

The program was entirely Italian music played by Italians. Mario Paci, the director of the Shanghai Municipal Orchestra played the piano, a tenor sang and a violinist played, but I must confess that my mind was not on the music. Opposite me, beside the high stone fireplace, sat a lovely little Chinese woman, another Mrs. Chu (the names Chu and Wong seemed to be as common as Smith and Jones in the States). This Mrs. Chu wore a cloth-of-silver modern Chinese dress with silver shoes and long diamond earrings, and sat very erect in a huge yellow upholstered, high-backed chair. At her right was the daughter of the French Consul, a slim blonde young girl with large brown eyes, wearing a peach-colored satin dress. These two women made a picture which might have been called East and West, and I suddenly realized that we were the only Americans there, and the only other English speaking people were Sir Frederick Maze, the British Foreign Head of the Chinese Customs, and Lady Maze. She was sitting on the right hand side of the room, very conservatively gowned in a dark green crepe dress with shoes to match, and I remember thinking that she would not have looked out of place sitting beside Queen Mary. Instead, beside her sat a small slip of a Chinese woman, with thin, fine aquiline features, Mrs. Wellington Koo. Her hair was brushed straight back from her forehead and she wore a coronet of gold wrought leaves like a halo, long diamond ear-rings, a dress of gold brocade, Chinese fashion with high collar and short sleeves, a double string jade necklace and beautiful jade and diamond rings, on long fingers that tapered to points, as her highly colored nails were a half inch long. Gold brocade modern evening sandals and a gold brocade hip-length cape of the same material as her dress and lined with sable, completed the ensemble. The cape, fur side out, was draped over the back of her chair, forming a perfect background for her shimmering costume. She sat very straight as if posing for a picture, and in fact was a perfect oriental miniature in gold cloth, jewels and sable. Mother told me later that she was considered the best dressed among the Chinese women, but was disliked for her snobbishness, by them also. Another illustration of how universal is feminine jealousy. I was told that she was the the daughter of a Straits Settlement Chinese of immense wealth, and that when he died, the family had a funeral of unheard of magnificence. A large steamer, an ocean liner, so the story goes, was bought and completely covered with fresh flowers. It was then sent out to an island with a large hill-side towards the sea, and that hill-side was also covered with fresh flowers, and he was buried there. His daughter certainly looked the part of my imaginary idea of a daughter of an oriental potentate!

I was thrilled by the contrasting types and nationalities, and although the music lasted until nearly midnight, I found the concert short. Food of the hors d'oeuvres type was then served and as usual all kinds of beverages. I talked to Mario Paci, the orchestra leader, a short, thin Italian with a kindly smile that illuminates his whole face. He holds a position of great esteem among the foreigners of the International Settlement. Every Sunday his Municipal Orchestra plays at the Lyceum Theatre, and in the summer evenings outdoors at Jessfield Park, the park that is run and supported by the Shanghai Municipal Council of the International Settlement.

A few evenings later I was invited to Mr. and Mrs. T. V. Soong's house for a reception and a showing of some movies which Mr. Soong as censor had forbidden for public presentation in Shanghai, but which he thought his friends might enjoy. At present Mr. Soong holds many positions in the Nationalist Government and is brother-in-law of President Chiang Kai-shek. Formerly he was Minister of Finance and is now head of the Bank of China and Advisor to the present Minister of Finance, H. H. Kung who is also a brother-in-law of the President. One picture was the "Lives of a Bengal Lancer," and as everyone knows the story, with war lords committing terrible deeds, one may imagine the reason for censoring it. The other picture was "The Notorious Mary Lang," a crook picture that showed very clever methods of theft. I might add that the talking parts of the pictures were all in English.

Mr. Soong's house was a large stucco-built two story mansion. The room where the pictures were shown, was on the ground floor, twice as long as the width, which was about thirty feet. Opposite the folding doors that led to the dining room, was a large portrait of Madame Soong, T. V. Soong's mother, and mother of all the now famous Soongs. The Soong family is of humble origin and not connected with any of the Manchus. This was Madame Soong's home, T. V. looks very much like her. He is about six feet tall, rather thick set, wears glasses and has a broad slavic face with complexion darker than the average Chinese. He talked very little but smiled pleasantly at everyone. Strangely enough his fingers were long and pointed, the sort one associates more with the artistic thinker than with the practical worker. I remember that current opinion was that he had more vision in his outlook for the future of the Chinese people, than many others who were in positions of equal influence in the present Nationalist Government.

His wife was lovely looking, tall and thin as Myrna

Loy, and not unlike her in features, although more distinctly Chinese. She wore her long bobbed hair straight back from her forehead and marcelled with ends all bushy and a circular comb holding it back. She was not as reserved as most Chinese women, and although she wore a modern Chinese dress, was more like a foreigner.

There were about twenty-five people there, none of whom I had met at the home of the Italian Ambassador, Count Lojacono. T. A. Soong, V. Soong's brother, who is in the Salt Service and resembles his brother not at all, being short, thin and talkative was most affable. Coffee and cakes were served and everyone stood stiffly around the large circular table laden with china and silver, in European style. No alcoholic beverages were served and everyone was working hard to make conversation.

After a short while we left, and I could hardly realize that I had just left the home of the famous T. V. Soong, had seen him in the flesh, and was complacently sitting back in the limousine, riding home through the electric-lighted streets of the French Concession, as from any ordinary evening party. Now almost a year later, I am just beginning to appreciate the variety of my contacts in Shanghai. One evening an Italian home, the next, a modern Chinese.

Soon afterwards I was entertained at dinner in an American home also in the French Concession. The hostess was the widow of a missionary who had died several years earlier, leaving her in very comfortable circumstances. Her married niece and nephew were living with her, and the house was beautifully furnished and modern. After the cordial conviviality of most homes in Shanghai, I felt the lack of cocktails, and was a bit constrained with twelve missionary minded people, even though they were Americans. Anyway, I must confess I was always disappointed when I found myself with Americans, it rather spoiled the atmosphere of foreign cosmopolitanism that I loved in Shanghai. After several conversational attempts, I was reduced to food as a topic, and asked a few questions about Chinese food, and was I answered! They told me about foods in the interior and southern parts of China and in Canton especially. Since then I have learned from trustworthy sources that their statements were not exaggerated. Delicacies are: unborn mice, served raw like oysters in covered cups like bouillon cups; monkeys' brain fluid, which is provided fresh by having a special table with holes big enough for live monkeys to stick their heads through; and by giving each one of the guests a hammer and spoon-like utensil with which they respectively crack the monkeys over the heads and help themselves to the fluid.

I heard another story from a well-known American woman coming back on the S. S. Coolidge about monkeys in Japan. She was loath to tell the story because she had told a college bred Japanese about it, and he was much perturbed and said he had never seen or heard anything like it in Japan. But her husband insisted upon her telling it because he said they had both seen it with their own eyes. The incident occurred in a small chemist shop, in a village through which they passed. As they entered the shop they saw on a counter at the back of the shop, a row of dried monkeys' heads, teeth and all. The Japanese in charge of the shop was grinding and pounding a dried head into a powder, and putting the powder in a small bag. They asked him the use of the powder and was told that when taken in water it would cure headaches. Not unlike the advice I was once given to eat poison ivy so that I should never run the chance of being poisoned again. Evidently there must be some oriental idea about the value of a monkey anatomy when taken internally. I've heard of monkey's glands supposed usefulness, but never monkey's brains.

The next delicacy mentioned, was snake's meat but one must eat three different kinds or risk ptomaine poisoning. Other choice tempters for jaded palate were bird's nest soup, shark's fins, duck skin fried crisp and dipped in a sour tasting sauce, and to top off the meal in place of a sweet, dried cockroaches. In Wing On's, a Chinese owned modern department store on Nanking Road, I saw a glass covered bowl with dried cockroaches in it, at three dollars Mex. for the pound, right beside bowls of dates, figs and almonds. Hearing about these strange foods did not add to my enjoyment of my dinner that evening.

While we were having after dinner coffee without the gentlemen, the others further heightened my gloom by discussing diseases and frightening experiences. I found out after a few weeks stay in Shanghai that these two topics were sure to crop up at every feminine social gathering. My hostess then told us about her recent trouble. She had just discharged her whole staff of household help, for she had discovered that the cook was going blind from a sex disease and all the rest of the help had it, even the Amah, nurse, who was taking care of her baby niece. Then they all talked about the thieves and how they barred the windows at night, although all the estates are completely surrounded with high walls with barbed wire on top and gates with heavy locks. One story told by the wife of a professor at Shanghai College, was about a young American woman missionary, whose hands were badly slashed by a coolie servant she had tried to discipline for laziness. That evening I was glad to return to the very modern Park Hotel, and I began to understand my mother's joy in the modernity and security of the hotel. I remember I locked my door very carefully that night and was extremely content to be up twelve stories.

But having heard so much about Chinese food, I was not as thrilled as I might have been, when a friend who had lived thirty years in China, invited me to a Chinese restaurant for dinner, and to see some of the night life of Shanghai afterwards. We went in his car with a Chinese chauffeur, to a restaurant on Nanking Road, Sun Ya, by name, frequented by foreigners as well as well-to-do Chinese. We entered a room that

looked like a hotel lobby of the eighteen ninety type.
Black walnut colored wood work and heavy leather
upholstered easy chairs, and I wondered where the
tables were. My friend led me up a wide marble
staircase at the rear of the room, to the second floor,
and I thought he had made a mistake and had taken
me to a beauty parlor, for the whole floor was divided
off into white curtained compartments. The Chinese
like privacy at meals, but I assumed, not necessarily
quiet. In the next compartment to ours, we heard a
party of Chinese men playing the finger game, my
friend explained. The idea is that one must guess how
many fingers the other man is going to hold up, and
shout it just before he raises his hand. If you lose, you
have to take another drink. By the sounds, I assumed
that everyone was losing.

The compartment where we were, had a mirror
across the back, a circular wood table with no cloth
and ordinary wooden chairs. On the side walls, were
hooks where our wraps were hung, and across the
front a white cotton curtain that the Chinese "boy"
meticulously pulled together each time he entered or
retired. I told my friend that I did not want to know
what I was eating, until afterwards. I was sure I could

eat whatever he could.

First of all a small basket was brought in, filled with hot wet Turkish towelling face cloths with which we were supposed to wash face and hands. My friend told me never to use the cloths in a public restaurant for they might be germy. Then the usual Chinese tea was served in covered cups, and our only departure from the Chinese meal, was a Manhattan cocktail after the tea. I found out afterwards that I had eaten bird's nest soup, which I remember, was delicious, if I do not allow myself to dwell on what I suppose were the ingredients, fried duck skin, the meat of the duck fixed like stew in a greasy gravy, rice, a dark colored sauce, soy bean sauce I learned later, that tasted very good on the crisp fried duck skin, a cooked fish, fish raw, a pudding like a cornstarch blanc-mange, very sweet and with a strong almond flavor, wine that tasted like a mild Sauterne but was potent, rice wine I learned later, and finally another departure from the Chinese meal, a brandy afterwards. I remember thinking that I was perhaps drinking too much of a mixture, but solacing myself with the thought that the alcohol would surely kill any poison I might have eaten.

All the food was set in the centre of the table, and

I learned that it was perfectly good form to reach forward and help yourself with your own chopsticks, and it makes no difference if you should spill food on the table in the process. Later I found that the centre of any Chinese table was apt to be quite spotted before a meal was half way through. This was my first Chinese meal, but not with Chinese people like the dinner I "experienced" later in Peiping.

This dinner was given by a Chinese gentleman in the Salt Service. It was a formal dinner served in the Chinese way with dishes of food in the centre of the table. The other guests were all Chinese. I found that it was perfectly good form to belch without apology, and that toothpicks were passed with the hot wet face cloths after dinner. During dinner, those cloths were brought frequently and I felt as if I were always wiping my face and hands. I especially remember that rice wine was served, because of the retired Chinese General opposite me. My host told me that General _____ was now the head of a secret espionage for Chiang Kai-shek, that he had been in many military campaigns on various sides and that he was honest too! The last part of the statement was made as if it were unusual for a general to be honest, which quite amused me. This General was an imposingly portly Chinese, and I should have been quite over-awed but for his manner which was most genial. He kept smiling at me and lifting his rice wine cup and saying "Gambei." The Chinese lady at my left explained that it meant to drain my cup of rice wine as he did. So I drank each time, thinking that I had to do it to be polite, and also because it helped me to keep my mind off what I was eating. After a time the lady next to me, smiled at my mother and said, "Your daughter has quite a capacity," and was my mother shocked! My mother should not have been shocked, I discovered later, for this comment was meant to be a compliment as it is considered a virtue "to have a capacity" without showing it. A moment later this same lady exclaimed to the host, "My, aren't you extravagant, shark's fins!" And she acted as if she were enjoying the anticipation. Another guest jocosely remarked, "What do you do with the rest of the shark?" Quick as a flash, the lady's husband, a most attractive young Chinese, answered, "We just catch them, and shave them, and throw them back into the water again." If they had not told me that the food before me was shark's fins, I should have thought I was eating thin spaghetti which had not been cooked enough. Just then the General across the table, belched a mighty belch and raised his rice wine cup to me, and no matter what anyone thought of my capacity, I drained my cup. There was a silence for a few seconds and out of the corner of my eye as I happened to glance behind me, I saw a mouse running towards the fireplace a few feet behind my host's chair. Convulsively I tucked my skirts tight between my knees and for once in my life was able to control my instinctive desire to jump up on a chair and shout when I see a mouse! Mother asked me after dinner what had made me look so distressed. She had not seen the mouse and had thought that something in the food had caused my perturbation, so I realized then how she felt about Chinese food herself. Anyway I remember feeling relieved that that mouse at least was not being served on that table. A silly thought because such a thing would not be likely to happen in Northern China. Only in Canton and the Southern Provinces are these strange kinds of meats served. But the young lady at my left had also noticed my perturbation, and laid it to embarrassment about table manners, so she kindly explained what was considered the correct thing to do at the table in China.

The host and hostess, with their own chopsticks put a little of everything on a guest's plate, as many as forty different kinds of food sometimes, but the guest need only taste each kind. Luckily forty different kinds of food were not served at that meal, as I had attempted to eat all that was put on my plate up to that time.

The General, having freely imbibed, became talkative, but as he could only speak Chinese, his evidently amusing anecdote would have remained a mystery but for the kindness of my host who told me the gist of the story after the General had finished. It was about the terrible eating habits of the Mongolians. He said that once when he was on a campaign in Inner Mongolia, during some peace negotiations, he had to eat a meal with them, and that a whole roasted animal was put in the centre of the table, and they all helped themselves by tearing off what they wanted with their hands. The General was offered a hunk of meat which he declined, so they gave him some wine. He did not take that either because the Mongolian who was pouring the wine had spit in the cup first, then wiped it around with his dirty finger to clean it, before pouring in the wine. It was very amusing to me to hear this Chinese General telling about the terrible eating habits of the Mongolians, and I was thankful that he could not know how strange his own habits seemed to me. It was really almost miraculous to me to see how cleverly they managed those slippery chop sticks. The hostess of this dinner was the woman who kept saying to me, "Poo-dung" which means "I do not understand you" while I talked on for a quarter of an hour. She also told me about her little boy who was then in the hospital having recently had an operation for a growth on his finger, because "it caused him so much pain to kick a ball with it." She meant his toe in place of his finger. I hate to think of the terrible errors I should make if I ever should have the courage to attempt to learn her language.

At another time in Shanghai, we were invited to tea in the home of a Chinese gentleman, Lord Li-Ching-Mai. Mother told me that I should consider myself very lucky to be invited there for many of her friends who had been in Shanghai for many years had never been invited to even a large party at Lord Li's home. We had been there for a cocktail party the Sunday before, and I was surprised that no other Chinese were present, although all the foreign Consuls and their wives, and other foreign government officials, including the Japanese were there. I asked someone about it and was told that Lord Li, being the son of Lord Li-Hung-Chang, belonged to the class sympathetic to the Manchus, hence was unpopular with the present Chinese government. His great wealth, inherited from his father, is erroneously considered ill-gotten because acquired during the rule of the Manchus. He in turn, has been badly treated by the Nationalist Government, his company the China Steam Navigation Co. has been confiscated, and since ruined by mismanagement and graft. After reading about the life and travels of Li-Hung-Chang, it was most interesting to be a guest of his son and family in their own home.

The next day at four we arrived and were shown into a small reception room opposite the front door, where we were greeted by Lord Li, his son Peter and his daughter-in-law, a slim pretty little Chinese woman. We sat down, Lord Li, opposite me in a high-backed chair, with his hands on his knees and his feet set wide apart, pointing outwards, the position accentuated by his white socks and black fabric Chinese shoes. Many Chinese gentlemen affect this position, I discovered later, just as American men sit back and cross their knees. The present Lord Li is about fifty years old and that afternoon wore the customary clothes of a Chinese gentleman, a long plum-colored heavy silk robe with a short black whipcord jacket with wide sleeves over it. His manner was open, demonstrative, contrary to my imagined picture of a Chinese gentleman. He spoke very fast in a deep toned voice, stammering a bit when searching for a word and using his hands as he talked.

To entertain us until the arrival of the other guests, Peter Li brought out some picture albums and laid them on a grand piano in a bay window of the reception room. Lord Li showed us pictures of his father, Li-Hung-Chang, and I had to pinch myself to realize that I was standing between the son and grandson of this famous gentleman. They showed photographs of him riding with the Kaiser Wilhelm II, in the Kaiser's crested Victoria with military escort; at the Elysee in Paris; with Victor Emmanuel in Italy; with Gladstone and Lord Salisbury in London; then a picture taken at West Point in 1910, of the cadets in review before Lord Li himself and Prince Ching, and another picture in 1924, of Lord Li, Peter Li, and the present puppet Emperor Pu Yi of Manchuria.

Just then the other guests were announced and I

was surprised to find that they were Americans, well-known in New York. Mr. and Mrs. ____ had with them another young woman who Mrs. ____ explained was the daughter of the President of the Standard Oil Co., and was travelling on the Empress of Britain with her father, who was speaking to the Company employees meantime. Lord Li had previously explained that the other expected guests for tea, had been given a letter of introduction to him, Lord Li, by his "very dear friend, Theodore Roosevelt, Jr." After the introductions were performed Lord Li, Peter Li and his wife led the way out into the garden. From the porch steps, a bed of hyacinths, blue and white, solidly in bloom, extended about two hundred feet long by fifty wide. A narrow stream of water ran through the middle with fountains playing at intervals. At the further end was a miniature pond that reflected the Chinese summer house beyond, surrounded by many cedars and odd shaped rocks typical of the Chinese gardens. We walked through the garden of rocks and many varieties of coniferous trees, and I was interested by the contrasting ideas expressed there, for at the end of one path was a white marble figure of a woman, and down another, an antique bronze idol.

To the left of this garden was a lawn about one hundred and fifty feet square with an open marble tea house at one end, at the other the "Ancestral Hall." Both were very much larger than I had expected. The Tea House had four marble steps about fifty feet long leading up to a terrace that length. It was about twenty feet deep, open on the sides except for the white marble columns, three feet in diameter, that supported the roof, thirty feet high. This white marble structure made a striking picture against the background of tall dark green cedars.

The Ancestral Hall, at the opposite end of the lawn, was white marble also, with marble columns across the front, supporting the overhanging third floor of the building. It was as long as the Tea House but fully forty feet from the front to the rear. At either side of the central door were large antique bronze urns. Inside this door one stepped into a central room thirty by fifty feet, with a ceiling two stories high. It was furnished with the most beautiful Chinese furniture, carved and inlaid with jade, and the walls were hung with Chinese lettered long embroidered satin banners, given to Li-Hung-Chang by the Emperor, honoring him for his services. Of the furniture I especially noticed a dining table that stood in the centre of the room. It was beautifully carved and inlaid, with the chairs to match. It was a round table about six feet across, and the seats of the chairs were made in the shape of a letter V, so that when all the chairs were unoccupied, they would fit together in a circle under the table, with the top of the chair backs making another circle of wood about three inches wide at the level of the table, so that it looked just like a table with no chairs.

On the first floor at the right of the main room, was Lord Li's study. His desk chair faced the lawn and gardens, and in front of the door behind his chair was the most beautiful screen that I have ever seen, inlaid with carved jade in varying shades of green and white. At the left was a small hallway with a narrow winding stairway, that did not correspond at all with the grandeur of the rest of the building, and of course there was no heat, as Chinese houses, no matter how expensive the furnishings, are never heated.

On the second floor was Lord Li's library, and here I was overcome by the American banker's behavior. Without asking permission, he opened a bookcase, took out a Chinese book in its wooden binding tied with tape, untied the tapes, laughed as he fingered the thin Chinese paper and said to Lord Li, "What's this all about?" Lord Li did not even smile and answered very quietly, which was unusual for him, "Those are letters from the Emperor to my father and of great value to me." His daughter-in-law tried to relieve the situation and said, "My father usually tells his guests that they must read all these books before he will show them the Hall for Sacrifices upstairs," but none of us laughed. We left the library silently and followed Lord Li up the narrow winding staircase to the top floor. The Hall for Sacrifices was a large room that occupied the whole of the top floor of the building. "Sacrifices" means celebrations of birthdays and deathdays of members of the family, I learned. On these days the picture of the member to be honored is hung in the hall and all the family do homage. What the homage was, I did not know then, but on my return I read that it is a symbolical service with a ritual, and various kinds of drum beating and candle burning, as strange to us as our communion service would probably appear to the average Chinese. At the time, I thought it would be rude to ask Lord Li about the ritual itself, but am sorry now that I did not get a first hand story from him.

At the back of the room was a long narrow table with two large red and gold drums standing at either end on wooden supports about three feet high. The wall was hung with large colored banners mostly red and gold, with Chinese characters on them. The first day we were there, a large scroll portrait of a grandmother was among them, showing that that day was her birthday. I did have the courage to ask how many generations back they went for celebrating birthdays and deathdays, for I was thinking, with the prolific Chinese families they would be doing nothing else but celebrate, if they went back far enough. Lord Li replied that they only commemorated the past three generations, and he further explained that especial honors were accorded the wives who had borne children. Someone asked about the monuments which one sees throughout the countryside for virtuous widows. Lord Li answered that if a widow never married again, her husband's family was bound to honor and care for her always and even put up a monument of an especial type for her after her death. The idea of being honored profusely after death and of having magnificent coffins and funerals is very important among the Chinese. I have been told that it is considered an especial filial act for a son to present his father with a fine coffin as a birthday present on his sixtieth birthday.

We left the Ancestral Hall and walked back through another beautiful Chinese garden of cedars and huge rocks to the conservatory at the right rear of the main house. There we were met by Lady Li, dressed in modern Chinese clothes. She was small and motherly looking, with her black hair brushed straight back from her forehead into a small knob at the nape of her neck. She cannot speak English, but has been around the world with Lord Li, who interprets everything. Nevertheless she presided. with gracious courtesy at the large round tea table which was set for ten people with red and silver chopsticks and a white cloth, in deference, I suppose, to her foreign guests. The table was in the centre of the conservatory, and the walls and all the framework of the windows were painted a Nile green. Plants were hanging from the ceiling, the feathery vines lending a more ornate and filmy appearance to the otherwise quite bare room, and flowering plants were massed against the wall towards the inner house. Mrs. Peter Li, the daughter-in-law excused herself, explaining that it was supper time for her children and she always stayed with them at that time. She joined us later and brought all four, two girls and two boys, the oldest eight and the youngest two. The youngest was named "Teddy" for his foreign name.

We then undertook the business of eating with chopsticks, and I've never tasted such delicious food. Among other things was lotus, "fresh from our garden" Lord Li explained, boiled, stuffed with cooked rice, chilled, coated with sugar and sliced. It was easy to pick up with chopsticks and was delicious too!

But I had by this time acquired a very good trick that I did not need to use this time, when I did not like the Chinese food. I would pick up food with the chopsticks and awkwardly drop it on the table, and in that way I had to eat very little. I told an American lady whose husband has been in the Chinese service for several years, about my scheme, and she warned me to be careful or I might have an experience like her sister's. At a dinner in the interior of China she tried my little trick, and an old gray-haired, kindly Chinese sitting opposite her, with "mossy teeth," felt so sorry for her that he carefully cleaned off his chopsticks by drawing them through his lips, then picked up a choice piece of meat with them from the centre dish and poked it into her mouth! It is considered perfectly good form among the Chinese to select a particularly nice morsel of food with your own chopsticks, and put it into the mouth of your friend. I never had that experience, but I kept a watchful eye on my dinner companions from then on.

While we were at the tea table at Lord Li's nothing odd or exciting happened until the intrusion of the Standard Oil Company in the person of the secretary of the President. He dashed into the room unannounced and said to the daughter of the President, "Hurry, or you'll miss the boat!" Lord Li was speechless with surprise, and I could imagine what he must have been thinking about this exhibition of American manners, or rather lack of them! With scant words of thanks and no apologies, the secretary and the daughter of the President departed hastily. Shortly afterwards we took our leave, escorted to the door by Lord and Lady Li, their son and his wife and their four little grandchildren.

The following Sunday morning we engaged a

Chinese guide and went to the Native City. Lord Li had assured us that there was no danger, except from pickpockets. He must have meant there was no danger for us, because I was told later that neither Lord Li himself nor any member of his family ever leaves his walled-in estate without armed guards, who travel in an automobile which precedes theirs. As I was not Lord Li, I felt I had nothing to fear, and was thrilled by the realization that I was actually in the Native City at last. Never have I heard such chattering voices and assorted kinds of noises, or seen so much dirt and so many people literally falling over each other. One of our party wanted to take some pictures of them, and pretended that I was the subject to be photographed. We had been told that some of the Chinese are superstitious about having their pictures taken, thinking it will bring them bad luck, but we got some good pictures of them for they were intently watching me while I posed.

There were bird markets with hundreds of birds for sale in all kinds of cages. Their singing made it seem as if there must be trees about, but not a tree or blade of grass or growing flower was in sight, just a few spindling potted plants for sale. Then we walked through countless narrow streets scarcely six feet wide. The buildings were mostly one story high, with shops open in front to the street, the family living in the rear. The houses were so close together that there was no room for grass or trees to grow. There may have been gardens and trees somewhere in the Native City but I did not see any.

The Chinese are very fond of birds, and many times even in the foreign section of Shanghai I would see a sedate Chinese gentleman, walking along the street, carrying a bird cage with his forefinger through a ring in the top, taking his pet bird for an airing, as we take our pet dogs.

Not far from an especially large bird market was the Confucian Temple reputed to be the oldest in China. The exterior was drab and dirty looking, but I thought the interior would be like the temples at Kioto in Japan, all gold and scarlet and clean. What was my amazement when I stepped inside to see an arcade of shops, with incense and paper syces and candles for sale! The roof was high and the whole interior was smoky and smelling of candle grease. The passages between the shops were narrow and crowded with people, who hawked and spit and chattered, while they trudged along the muddy floors. I was thoroughly disillusioned! We mingled with the crowd and going down a narrow passage with walls about six feet high, we came upon a huge gilded awful-looking image about twelve feet high, with a terrifying expression on its face. It was hidden on three sides by dirty dull colored velvet curtains, but visible at the front opening. It sat on a platform just at the level of my eyes, and the people approached in single file and put their paper offerings at its feet.

Down another narrow passage were more awful-looking ugly gold and red painted, man-sized images, four seated in a row. The guide said that they were for the servants to worship and by now I was ready to believe anything. Certainly this place was not the haven of peace and rest I had imagined a Confucian Temple would be! To further heighten my impression of sordidness, I was told that the priests carried on a profitable business, by buying the daily garbage from the big hotels and restaurants in the foreign section, and selling it to the people near the temple for food. It seemed to me that if this story were true, the garbage must be very good fare, for the people I saw looked very well-fed.

Finally we moved on out of the Temple, if one must call it that, and saw a Chinese standing in front of a tent-like booth intoning in a sing-song voice, the way they all do when they are calling out their wares. (Usually there are two men who carry on an antiphonal duet that is really very pretty to hear.) This man beckoned to us and we realized he had a show inside. The fee paid, in we went! Several monstrosities were exhibited on a high platform opposite the entrance, and the nearest to me was a leering misshapen idiot child with drooling mouth. I could not get out of that place fast enough! I was horrified that a show of human unfortunates could be tolerated opposite a temple.

We wandered through more narrow streets, swarming with Chinese of all ages and types. I remember particularly a beautiful boy about twelve years old, with white skin and dark curly hair but dressed like a Chinese boy. I was told that he probably had a foreign father. It gave me an unhappy feeling to see him there speaking and acting like the Chinese children, supremely unconscious of the strangeness of his appearance in those surroundings, and of the probable unhappiness of his future. Eurasians are outcasts from both the yellow and the white races.

At length we came to the famous Spirit Bridge that leads to the reputed oldest tea house in China, the Willow Pattern Tea House. The bridge forms a right angle with the tea house at the apex, and crosses a muddy body of water with all kinds of refuse floating on the surface. There are several small right angle turns in each large angle of the bridge, made that way to keep away the evil spirits, as evil spirits are supposed to travel in a straight line. I had seen many photographs of this bridge and tea house, and had expected to be charmed by the beautiful symmetry of the architecture. The lines were there, but the photographs did not show the dirt, rotting wood and strong smells. That day, Sunday, the tea house was filled to overflowing as was the bridge at either side. There was a fight going on and the Chinese police were just arriving, so we did not go in.

We walked all the way across the bridge to the street at the other side. A crowd was gathered there intently watching something. We edged our way through and saw on a small raised screen about three or four feet above the heads of the people, animated pictures of the destruction at Chapei and pictures of corpses and general carnage. The crowd watched silently and I wondered if they understood this potent propaganda against the Japanese.

A few blocks beyond, at a small shop, the only funny incident of the morning occurred. I saw some small silvery-looking figures on horse back, done in relief, and I thought they would be wonderful for radiator ornaments for our cars at home. After the usual bargaining with the guide interpreting, I bought two, and then asked him what they represented. With some embarrassment he explained that brides hung them over their beds to bring babies. I decided then that they would not be suitable ornaments for automobile radiators. It was nearly noon so we left the Native City, and went back to the waiting automobile, having purchased many things from kites shaped like big birds, bamboo pipes a yard long, to rhinestone hair ornaments.

Another Sunday, in a Chinese section of the International Settlement, I had another amusing experience. When I told mother's Chinese chauffeur that I wanted to go to a shop where I could have a coolie suit made for myself like the blue denim street cleaner's suits, he looked at me as if I had lost my mind. We drove to a shop open to the street which had coats and pants hung across the front. When I got out of the car and went in, there was a great jabbering in Chinese. After the first excitement subsided, the chauffeur explained that I wanted to be measured for a Chinese man's coat, which request was received with looks of astonished incredulity, but finally they consented to take the measurements, "Chinese way" the chauffeur explained, when I was surprised to have them measure the length of my arm, starting from the centre of my back to my wrist. After all the measurements were taken but the neck, there was an embarrassing silence and they all stood about furtively looking at each other and me. I asked the chauffeur what was the trouble, and he said, averting his eyes and pointing to his own neck. "What size?" I threw open my fur coat for them to measure and, to my astonishment, they all looked away and did nothing! After another embarrassing pause I pulled my coat together. Immediately everything was all right again and they all started jabbering. I paid a deposit and went back to the car. Mother explained the incident, by telling me that it was considered very immodest for a Chinese woman to show her neck hence the embarrassment of those poor Chinese when I threw open my coat. After that I naturally noticed every Chinese woman's neckline and I never saw the most modern Chinese woman nor even a coolie woman, without a high collar, although their skirts are often slit way above the top of their long stockings. On my return crossing on the S. S. Coolidge, I was interested to see the way some Chinese women in the second class were dressed. They had evidently become aware that their legs were noticeable, for they wore starched white lace petticoats which came to their ankles underneath their straight slit-skirted Chinese dresses. If I had known enough to be tactful in Shanghai, when going to the Native quarters I should have worn a high lace yoke in my dress, I suppose! What is considered modest in different countries is a very interesting subject. Going over on the S. S. Hoover, Dr. Koo, a Chinese well-known in the states for his tolerance, in a talk explaining some differences between the Chinese and Americans in ideals of behavior, said that the Chinese consider it very bad form to show any emotion in public. He said that although a Chinese girl and boy might be very much in love, they would never hold hands or show the least sign of affection in public, and added that it gave him, with all his experience away from China, "goose pimples up his back," when he saw a man and girl kiss each other even in the movies. He also spoke of the interesting fact, that love stories and poems in Chinese are only written about married people.

In contrast to these sentiments of physical modesty was a sight I saw from the train window near a country village on the Great Northern Plain en route to Peiping. Awaking early I pulled up the curtain of my berth window and saw several Chinese men squatting down along the bank of a stream with their naked posteriors exposed to view, answering a call of nature, while they nonchalantly looked over their shoulders at the passing train.

My next adventure was to go riding through the section of the Chapei district which had been bombarded by the Japanese. A Colonel with the U.S. Army, who was in France during the World War, said that the loss of life and destruction in Chapei had been worse than any destruction he had seen in France. After seeing how crowded the other native sections are, I could imagine the horror that a single shell could create! This Chapei section is now mostly rebuilt and several Japanese live there. There is a large Japanese arsenal as well, where there has been nightly gun practice ever since the bombardment two years ago, which must sound decidedly ominous to the Chinese who still live there.

From there we drove on to Kiangwan, the section where the "New City" has been planned under the supervision of the present Mayor Wu-Te-Chen. He is one of the Cantonese faction which was unpopular with Chiang Kai-shek a few years back. But his loyalty to the principles of Sun Yat Sen, his honesty and efficiency have made him a strong power in the present Nationalist Government. He had sent invitations to mother for the first trial of a mass marriage, his own idea. This experiment is an attempt to change some of the ancient marriage customs, and is regarded with scepticism by conservative Chinese. With mass marriage the mothers of the brides are relieved of the terrible financial burden formerly put upon them. In many cases the mothers had been forced to labor excessively for the rest of their lives to pay the debt necessarily incurred by their daughters' marriages, I was told.

Mother and I had seats in the front row, Mrs. Wu-Te-Chen and Mrs. Wellington Koo were in the row behind us. The French Consul and his wife, and an American newspaper reporter, were the only others besides ourselves who were not Chinese. The centre of the hall was left vacant and at either side about two thousand Chinese were seated facing the stage. Suddenly a band at the back of the hall, started to play Lohengrin's Wedding March, and the glass doors at the rear were thrown open, and the brides in pairs on one side and the grooms on the other filed into the hall and stood facing the stage in two long lines. It gave me a most confused feeling to hear that familiar music and to see fifty Chinese brides and fifty Chinese grooms in place of one American bride and groom. The brides wore white net wedding veils with orange blossoms like American brides and white silk or satin modern Chinese style dresses with the inevitable high collars, short sleeves and skirts slit up the sides to the knees. They all carried large bouquets of pink carnations. The grooms wore long dark colored Chinese coats, slit at the sides showing dark pants tied around the ankles.

They went up four steps to the stage, and were married two couples at a time. A bas-relief portrait in bronze of Sun Yat Sen was on the rear wall of the stage, and they bowed to it three times thereby pledging

themselves to the doctrines of Sun Yat Sen, three times
to each other and three times to Mayor Wu-Te-Chen
who was standing at one side. It took exactly three
minutes to marry two couples at a time. After being
married the couples stood together in a third line
facing the stage. You may figure how long they had
to stand there, as there were fifty-two couples to be
married at three minutes for every two couples! I read
later that the Chinese as a race have great endurance
and after seeing that marriage I can well believe it.
When they were all married, they filed out of the
hall through the big glass doors through which they
came and down the wide steps to the lawn two stories
below. The audience or guests I should say, left by
an inside staircase leading through the office part of
the building. So I saw the first Mass marriage, which
I think will be considered by future generations one
of the important landmarks in the building of "New
China." It was interesting, I thought that this new
building, The Civic Centre, where the marriage took
place, was designed by a native of New England, Mr.
Henry Killum Murphy. The whole Kiangwan section,
newly built with broad macadam roads and sewerage,
was the most heartening sight in all of the China I saw,

although of course not as interesting as the old Native City.

My next adventure was a tour of Shanghai by night with an ex-Methodist minister who loved to dance. His wife was ill with the flu, and could not entertain me so wanted her husband to do the honors. She was a most interesting woman, and before her marriage had been an interpreter at the Court of the Empress Dowager. We started about seven and went to a Russian restaurant, "Kavkaz," which had the usual superfluity of messy Russian food, and to add to my discomfort I learned that my escort was a teetotaler, so I did not have a cocktail! After dinner we attended the premiere performance of some Balinese dancers at the Carlton Theatre. Some of them not over twelve years old had been trained from infancy to do these dances, and this was the first time they had ever performed outside their native land. Their whole technique of dancing was quite different from our western idea, and seemed to be an attempt to show how limber and supple they were. One particular jerking motion of the head was most ludicrous and not at all beautiful. The costumes and stage setting were not authentic Balinese, but were just the same, a bizarre contrast to

the theatre, which was a replica of any American Play
House built in the eighteen nineties!

After the theatre we went to the Paramount, a
combination night club and dance palace. It had been
recently built by the Chinese bankers and was ultra
modern in design with lots of nickel and crystal and
white woodwork. A circular white marble staircase
led up to the main dance floor. On the balcony over the
entrance, there was another dance floor, but made of
glass with electric lights under it, which made me feel
as if I were dancing on eggs. On the stage at the end
of the hall opposite the entrance, was the orchestra.
It was Russian, but played all the latest American
jazz. We arrived just as the floor show began. The
chorus girls were Russians also, and several were
blonde. Their costumes were scant, hats, slippers and
a very minute loin cloth. They danced not too well
compared with American chorus girls, and sang the
latest American songs in broken English. I was told by
an English friend that the Russian girls can be hired
cheaper than the Chinese and that the Chinese admire
blonde white women. To illustrate he told me about
two young Chinese men, working in a bank, who had
an opportunity offered by rich relatives to go to the

States for a few years experience in U. S. banking, whose one expressed desire, was to possess a blonde white woman!

All nationalities were there that night, the daughter of the French Consul as well as Mrs. Wellington Koo, the latter accompanied by two other Chinese women in Chinese style dress, and three foreign men in tuxedos! At two in the morning we left the Paramount and started for "French Town." It was very foggy and I did not relish the idea of driving way out in the French Concession in the middle of the night, but away we whirled! I remember thinking that the ex-minister seemed to know his way around Shanghai at night very well the way he drove along through that dense fog. We turned into a dark driveway, thickly wooded at either side, and came to a dimly lit doorway, which was opened for us. We stepped into a small dingy hallway, and I made up my mind not to check my coat. In the next room there was a long bar crowded with people, and the room beyond was gaudily decorated in gold and white. An orchestra was playing on a small stage and people were dancing in the centre of the room. On one side there were small tables for two where the paid dance girls sat, all of them Russians or Eurasians, the majority again blonde, and dressed in European style clothes. Behind them was a long bench against the wall where several men were sitting. When the music started to play, these men picked out a girl and several other men at the tables around the other sides of the room, did likewise. But the moment the music stopped playing, they left the girls in the middle of the floor to find their own way back to the tables, which seemed very strange to me. It was explained that the men have to pay for each piece of music played, if accompanied by one of the girls, whether they dance or not! I figured there certainly must be a depression on among the dancing men of Shanghai because they were leaving the girls so speedily after each dance. I was told the girls receive very small fees and consider themselves lucky if they are ever invited to sit at a table with a man customer. A very stout entirely bald German had a small half-fed-looking blonde girl sitting at his table for most of the time I was there, although he did not dance but drank and ate with her. Several well-dressed Chinese women were dancing with paid dance girl partners, learning to do modern dancing that way. Mrs. Wellington Koo's party arrived soon after we did, and many well-known foreigners were sitting at the tables. Del Monte's, the name of this establishment, takes especial pride in serving, what they called American style ham and eggs, for five o'clock breakfast. At three thirty I thought I had seen all I wanted of Shanghai's night life, different in only one respect from all other night life I have seen; all nationalities were there.

But at another time I saw more night life, and went to the Majestic among other places, a night club on Bubbling Well Road. There all the paid dance girls are Chinese, as are most of the patrons. The girls were very pretty and wore Chinese modern dresses in all colors of the rainbow. Their slim boyish figures, a physical characteristic of all young Chinese women, were accentuated by the straight lines of the Chinese style dresses. They all had their hair bobbed and marcelled, wore long earrings and used much make-up. There were very few foreigners there that evening and no foreign women. The foreign men were dancing with the Chinese girls, and the orchestra, again Russian, played only American Jazz. It was most surprising to see those Chinese young men and women, in Chinese clothes dancing in position and steps exactly like our most up to date youngsters in America!

The girls sat at tables for two encircling the entire dance floor as large as the Paramount floor but with no overhanging balconies. The customers sat at tables just behind the girls. I was told that at both Del Monte's and the Majestic, the girls are taken home in motor busses after closing hours, a rule they must follow or lose their jobs.

Another evening I went to Hai-a-Lai, an indoor arena like the Boston Garden only not as large of course. There I had a marvelous chance to see the Chinese in a state of gambling excitement. They bet on the players, professionals from South America, and as they grew more excited, their voices rose in pitch, so that they sounded more like a crowd of women than men. It was a revelation to sit among that shrieking, excited crowd of Chinese. I could not keep my attention on the players, any more than I could at the first wrestling match I ever saw in America, and I must say that the Chinese crowd looked far less ugly than a wrestling match audience. Before I went to China I had read many accounts of the extreme actions of the Chinese when gambling. One particular story in Ralph Townsend's book published in 193– ,"Ways That are Dark," quoted from one of several tales, by Abbe Huc, was that the Chinese would even bet one of their fingers after they had lost everything else, and if they lost, would actually cut off the forfeited finger. Quoting Mr. Townsend, "Huc relates that the gambling halls there at the time (there, being a town not far from the Great Wall) commonly kept a hatchet, a block, and a bowl of hot oil. The hot oil was to cauterize the spot where the finger had been cut off." I must confess that I believed this might really be so, and was much relieved when I read, since my return from China, in a book published in England in 1860, "Pictures Of The Chinese," by the Rev. R. H. Cobbold, this same story of Abbe Huc's without Mr. Townsend's scenic embellishments, referred to, as a "Ridiculous account evidently founded upon the near resemblance in sound of two Chinese phrases, "To chop off a finger," and "To draw a lot," which latter is a common mode of gambling. If mistakes like this can be made with the Chinese language by a man as famous as Abbe Huc, and repeated in all gravity by a man of Mr. Townsend's standing, I feel that many other stories about Chinese cruelty may rest on as thin a foundation and therefore should be considered as sceptically as stories of atrocities during the World

War.

There is a great difference between the high-class and coolie Chinese in the tone pitch of their voices, or else it was just coincidence that the educated Chinese I saw had deeper voices. I saw many Chinese bankers at the Park Hotel, going to and from business banquets, or with ladies. They appeared in voice and manner as conservative as Boston's best, and their funny custom of shaking their own hands when they greet each other, further creates an impression of self-contained reserve. I shall never forget my surprise when I saw for the first time, two Chinese gentlemen greet each other pleasantly and then both shake their own hands! All I could think of was the expression "hugging oneself with delight."

3

TRIP TO PEIPING/PEKING

Everywhere I went I was asked two questions, how I liked Shanghai, and whether I had seen Peiping, adding that if I had not, I had not seen China. My mother had lived there for a time and thought I should see it. Maps were brought out and I was shown how we should go by train, through Soochow, Nanking and then north across the Great Northern Plain, through the provinces of Amohei and Shantung, crossing the Grand Canal at Suchowfu, stopping at Pengpu, Kuchen, Luchen, Teng-hsien, Yenchowfu, Chu-fou, Tawen-kow, Tsinan-fu, Tientsin and a lot of other places. It was suggested that we return by a more inland route, and visit "Jimmy Yen" of the new Chinese alphabet fame, whom my family knew well, and then down to Hankow and from there by river boat back to Shanghai, taking two days and one night on the boat alone. Mother and I were not very enthusiastic, as it would mean Chinese accommodations all the way back, and the idea was given up when we heard there was plague at a place not far from Hankow.

We left Shanghai at four, one Friday afternoon, on the Shanghai-Peiping express. It was far from being an express, as it went about twenty-five miles an hour so that we arrived in Peiping Sunday at noon. The compartments of the Wagon-Lits were modern and comfortable and there was a dining car on the train but we had been advised not to eat there so we had taken all our food with us for the thirty-six hour trip. Boiling water was brought to us by the porter at any time of day or night, and boiled water, cooled in corked bottles, could be bought from him also. At either end of the sleeping cars, was a fully armed Chinese soldier, and at every station any white passengers who stepped out on the platform were carefully watched. At one small place mother hopped off alone and she said afterwards that the soldiers immediately ranged themselves in a sort of a half circle separating her from the Chinese on the platform. If you ask about danger of attack by bandits, you are assured there is nothing to fear. But I kept remembering the stories I had read about bandits riding on trains as ordinary passengers, and I hated to get up in the night and see an armed Chinese soldier peering in the door at the end of the car. They looked so sinister in the half light that it gave me a very squeamish feeling.

In every small hamlet there were fortified towers as well where people went in case they were attacked by bandits. The villages looked very much the same, some larger than others, with groups of one story mud huts with straw roofs. I did not see at any time during the two days train ride any land that was not in use either for cultivation or for burials, and at no time could I look over the landscape without seeing a tombstone. The "Great Northern Plain" was hilly much to my surprise, and the hills were denuded of trees. I was told that every tree had been cut for firewood for centuries, and that none had been planted which is one of the causes of the terrible floods. The poverty of the population is hard to understand, for the land is fertile and yields two crops a year to one of ours in the States. It was explained that the farmers could live in plenty, if they were not exploited by the leaders of a pernicious Guild system. In one branch of production, out of the amount paid for the produce, sixty per cent is filched by the Guild executives and only the remaining forty per cent is left for the farmers. This system of exploitation has gone on for centuries. Many times the people have revolted, but inevitably were unsuccessful. Their leaders always disappeared. After centuries of this treatment, the result is a class of completely cowed and domesticated individuals. This system of mysteriously eliminating the leaders of any opposition to the powers that be, is a common method of crushing reform among the Chinese but this gangster method is equally common in certain European countries today. It was rumored that the present President of the Nationalist Government is not above using these Dictator methods. At one time when his supremacy was threatened by the progressive Cantonese group, he went to Shanghai, joined all their societies, craftily learned the names of the ring leaders, and then with the help of foreign capital, secretly arrested about two thousand of them and had them beheaded. It was rumored that the present Mayor of Shanghai, Mayor Wu-Te-Chen, was one of those who escaped. Several of the young Chinese who had high hopes of great social reforms for the Chinese people, were spiritually completely crushed by this coup, among them, the famous Dr. Hu Shih, the present Dean of Peiping University. My mother knew him well and said that he was a fine man. Just before I left Shanghai, he came to the Park Hotel. He was in Shanghai then to attend the meetings of the China Foundation Committee which administers the Boxer Indemnity money for the benefit of China. Relative to this Indemnity money it interested me to hear that there is much doubt expressed by the foreign population, whether the Chinese will keep on appropriating, out of their government revenue, the sum necessary to continue the running of the Indemnity Fund Institutions, all, of course, for the benefit of the Chinese people, after the termination of the time for the Indemnity Fund payments from America, which is about five years from now. I was also told that much that we hear about the "New China" is propaganda to satisfy, for the time being, the radical Chinese; that the present government is making a pretense of sympathizing with the "New China" movement, but has made no sincere attempt for reform. The pernicious practice of extortion under the Guild system has not been disturbed. In certain Guilds the executives have recently much advertised the fact that there is a fairer division of profits, but upon investigation it was found that they were now taking but forty per cent of the profits as opposed to their sixty per cent formerly. I was told that the attitude of those in power in the government today is, that nothing can be permanently accomplished until peace is established, and peace, to be enforced, as it has to be in China today, is financially and humanly expensive. It was said that although President Chiang Kai-shek was a ruthless military dictator, that his desire to keep peace and order at any cost, justified the means he employed to bring them about; and that he has extensively used the army to build roads especially in Kiangsu Province where he subdued the Communists.

In most of China today there are no roads, only muddy footpaths, which are adequate for the primitive methods of transportation still in use. Loads are carried on donkeys or on either end of bamboo poles balanced on the shoulders of the carrier, woman or man. As for the primitive farming methods of the Chinese, these have been recounted many times, and their way of keeping the same land fertile for generations, the nightly spreading of human manure, "night soil."

Sunday morning I looked out of the train for hours at mud huts with straw roofs always the same, at people in drab-colored ragged clothes, laboring with primitive farm implements; at hundreds of burial mounds, mute symbols of the generations who had lived and died in these same surroundings. Night soil — fertile crops — food consumed — night soil — an endless depressing cycle of activity for the past thousands of years! I felt as if we would never reach Peiping, that we were going to ride on forever surrounded by barren hills, myriad burial mounds, and these thousands of drab clothed Chinese people, but suddenly I saw in the distance a square looking high stone edifice, and before I realized the train was going through it and we were in Peiping. A Chinese friend of my Mother, had succeeded in engaging rooms for us at the Grand Hotel de Peking, otherwise we should have had to stay at a missionary's house in the Chinese city. After the long train ride I had no desire to be in romantically native surroundings, as I had on my arrival in Shanghai!

That afternoon we went out of the city about three miles to the Empress Dowager's Summer Palace, and found that it was open to the public at a reduced rate that day, so there were crowds of Chinese people of all classes. They behaved much the same as a Sunday crowd in Central Park enjoying the beautiful surroundings. It was hard to believe that the high hill on which the main buildings were built and the large lake in front, were artificially made, and the thought of the back-breaking labor this pile of wood and stone represented, rather dulled my appreciation of the architectural splendors. So although my imagination, stimulated by the gorgeous relics, crumbling remains and anecdotes I heard about the Summer Palace, could paint for me an alluringly dazzling picture of fairy tale oriental splendor, I was far from displeased by the crowds of drab costumed people enjoying themselves, and thronging the buildings and the paths along the lake where formerly only despots walked! I was intrigued by one young man evidently a student who with a small Brownie camera was taking a close-up picture of an early single blossom on a Magnolia tree, and again by the spectacle of several small boys climbing all over a statue of a large Peking lion that was on the terrace just above the long covered walk, where we were told the Empress Dowager and her

Court ladies used to take a daily promenade, along the shores of the artificial lake. Visible about a mile distant across this lake is the Jade Pagoda, built on a natural hill. The spring from that hill has supplied the water for Peking for thousands of years. No wonder they built a monumental pagoda on top of it!

At Yen Ching University where we next stopped, there is a beautiful modern built pagoda that surrounds a water tower, and all the buildings are modern in construction and materials, but strictly Chinese architecturally. They were designed by the same architect, Mr. Henry Killam Murphy, who designed the Civic Centre in Shanghai which I have already described and were paid for by Rockefeller money. One of the gentlemen whom I knew in Shanghai was in charge of the administration of the building fund. Dr. Layton Stewart is the present President, but he was not at home when we were there. I met him later in Shanghai. His house is a perfect example of a modern Chinese house, I was told, and I should love to have one just like it!

The next day I saw another Chinese house when we called on Mr. and Mrs. Chien Chen. Their parents were wealthy silk merchants, so both had been educated in the States. We called in the early forenoon and were shown into the living room just off the main hallway. The gentleman in our party was invited to take the seat of honor. It was a large double chair with an arm running through the centre from the back to the front, and it was on a platform raised about a foot above the floor level. I was told that only one side was ever used, so as to show that no one else in a gathering was worthy to sit in as exalted a position as the honored guest. Tea was then served, an inevitable occurrence in a Chinese house no matter what time of day one might call, and their four little children were introduced to us. Their mother was much pleased by our surprise when each child spoke to us in English, a courtesy that I could hardly imagine in an American home, for a visiting Chinese. Their house was particularly interesting to me for I was told that it had belonged to the Duke of Wei, the father of the Empress Dowager. I was equally intrigued by the fact that the Chens had put in central heating among other renovations, for Chinese houses rarely have heating systems. I have a vivid memory of dining at one Chinese home, wearing my fur coat over my evening gown!

That afternoon we went to the Temple of Heaven

and it is beautiful architecturally although made of wood. It is literally rotting away because the Chinese Government has no money to keep it in repair. The next morning we went up Coal Hill and had a beautiful view of the Forbidden City in the early morning sun. The golden roofs in yellow tile looked most alluring, but when we went down into the buildings later, and saw the dust, dirt and crumbling decay, I wished I had been content to let my imagination picture the reputed splendor of the interiors. Distance lent enchantment to most of the beauty spots I saw in Peking. But I was interested to see the priceless collection of works of art, precious stones, and the famed collection of clocks although they were not made by the Chinese but sent as gifts to the Emperors from all over the world. Volumes have been written about Peking and the beauties of the Summer Palace, The Temple of Heaven, The Forbidden City, but the destitute, dusty, thickly populated districts through which one passes to reach them, have been lightly stressed. Rows of one story dried mud huts line the narrow dirt streets through which the "Peking dust", a dry yellow dust as fine as coal ashes, swirls in clouds, and not a blade of grass, or tree or flower grows anywhere near these miserable dwellings. On the way to the Temple of Heaven, the Chinese gentleman who was taking us about in his limousine, pointed out an ancient beheading block in a square, where he said the Emperors used to hold public executions! When I was at the Temple of Heaven I tried hard to imagine the grandeur of the scene of the Emperor and his Court, dressed in gorgeous Chinese robes going in an impressive procession at dawn to worship, but in the back of my mind was the picture of his miserable subjects and their descendants today. Peking the beautiful everyone called it, to me it was Peking the terrible! A colossal monument to the vanities and oppressions of a long line of tyrants, with the present poverty stricken, disease ridden generation the result! I could not help but wonder whether the Chinese masses today might not be better off today, controlled by Japanese than exploited by their own race. Quite innocently I expressed this opinion to a group of various kinds of foreign nationals and was told that if the Japanese were in control they would eventually exclude all other foreigners, and as much foreign capital is invested in China, the Japanese must not be allowed to dominate. The money motive again, I thought, the determining factor in international

relations. But these same people admitted that the
Japanese give more in return to the Chinese in civic
improvements for the gains derived by them than the
other nationals. Among the foreign nationals there are
all classes of people whose race is often their only point
of contact. The day before we left Peiping, mother
had a sore tooth. She had lived in Peking for several
months a year or so ago, when Mr. ____ of recent
Addis Ababa fame was in the American Consulate,
so she knew of an American dentist in whose work
she had faith, although she told me that I must pay
no attention to his queer ideas. When we arrived at
his office, upstairs on the second floor of a modern
building in the legation quarter of Peiping, strains of
soft music greeted us. While mother was having her
tooth examined, the music continued and the dentist
told us that he always had soft music playing while
he worked, for he felt that a harmonious atmosphere
had a soothing effect on his patients. I was sorry for
mother if he felt his dentistry was so bad that he had
to have music to help him. With apparent relish at the
idea of a new audience he expounded his pet theory,
aesthetic living. He told us that we should surround
ourselves with an aura of beauty so that all our lives

might be lived aesthetically. After many preambles, he reached the crux of his theory, an explanation of his cult of aesthetic love. The two Chinese dentists who were assisting him, handing him each sterilized instrument as he examined mother's tooth, furtively were watching the effect of his words on the white woman. I was standing at the other side of the dentist's chair, saying not a word for fear I might stop the flow of oratory, for I could not wait to hear what he was going to say next. When mother could free her mouth she asked naïvely if his cult was the same as nudism. He lifted up his hands in horror and told us that nudists had no idea of aesthetics, for they allowed themselves to be exposed in all of their natural ugliness, whereas those belonging to the cult of aesthetic love, took hours to paint their bodies white like statues, and practiced for days to assume the most beautiful poses. Aesthetic love was a "thing of the mind" and had nothing to do with physical contact. I wished afterwards that I had asked him how one could propagate the race, as an aesthetic lover, but he had fixed mother's tooth temporarily, and I was somewhat benumbed mentally by his dose of aesthetic love to the accompaniment of soft music and the fragrance of antiseptics, so for once in my life I kept quiet! Mother told me afterwards that he had had a wife and three children before he became an aesthetic lover, and his wife had left him because of his cult, so I figured out he had done his propagating before he became aesthetic! Among other tales he told us was one about some missionaries who had recently attacked his cult as immoral, but had since become aesthetic lovers themselves. It was hard for me to imagine any missionaries I had ever seen, being beautiful enough to qualify as nude members of an aesthetic cult, but I was beginning to believe that one could find anything in China, even missionaries as aesthetic lovers! He emphasized the fact that he did not believe in free love, but believed that "love must be free." It all sounded rather fishy to me and I felt much as Fanny Brice, in her famous skit in The Follies, at a nudist camp when she said that "she found that Doctor was a snake in the grass." Well, it takes all kinds of people to make a world and this dentist has a very good reputation as a dentist in Peiping. I thought afterwards that maybe one of the missionaries converted to the cult had been suffering from a toothache and had been relieved by the aesthetic dentist. I could understand conversion under those circumstances! He recommended another dentist unknown to mother in Shanghai, and I was much amused when he warned us that we should probably think the other dentist very peculiar, because he quoted poetry while he worked, but was all the same a genius in dentistry. Evidently the atmosphere of the Orient does queer things to dentists.

4

LAST DAYS IN SHANGHAI AND DEPARTURE

WE LEFT PEIPING in one of the famous dust storms. Mr. and Mrs. Tseung, the Chinese people who entertained us at the dinner I described earlier, came to the train to see us off. I had a hard cold that was aggravated by dust, and which prevented me from being disturbed by the odors from the night soil that so many people complain about in the Chinese countryside. I was really very fortunate for the ride back as the two days and three nights were hot and dusty, and the clean and modern equipped Park Hotel in Shanghai, was a welcome relief! But here at home over a year later, my memories of Peking have become mellow, and I think of the places I saw, as I see them in highly colored photographs, cleansed of the dust and unpleasant contemporary associations. I think if I ever go to Peking again, I shall understand the glamor that others say they feel for the crumbling remains of a past splendor.

The following Sunday we were invited to the French Club for the regular Sunday afternoon tea dance. The dance floor was on the second floor and a white marble staircase led up to it at the right of the main entrance. The room was built in a large oval shape with a very high circular roof, and around the oval dance floor, tables were arranged in lines five deep at the long sides of the oval. The orchestra, Russian, and playing modern jazz, was on a stage at the end of the floor opposite the entrance. There were seven other people in our party, all Americans, and the hall was crowded with all nationalities, but I do not remember any Chinese. Afterwards I went to the Bar, the famous "Bar at the French Club," as the magazine FORTUNE described it. From the point of view of beauty, it was a disappointment, very long and made of dark mahogany, like any bar in an hotel of the 1890 type. There were small tables all over the rest of the room which was as large as a small dance hall, and these tables were filled with foreigners of all nationalities. Before the World War this building belonged to the Germans, and after the war the French confiscated it.

From there we went to Sir Frederick and Lady Maze's home for cocktails. Everyone there except ourselves were English people of the extreme type, and the house was a marvel of Britishness! Opposite the entrance door, at the back of a hallway about fifteen feet in depth and fifty feet in length, was a beautiful model of a Chinese junk about four feet in length, inside a heavily carved ebony and glass case. At the left side of the hallway, was an oil painting in a wide carved ebony frame, about five by six feet, of an enormous yellow and black tiger, showing his teeth and looking as if he were about to bound out of the picture! On the floor in front, was a huge yellow and black tiger skin rug, the tiger who was originally in it, having been shot by Sir Frederick in India his wife explained. The tiger skin, the Chinese junk, the Chinese servants in their long white coats with bright yellow short silk jackets, the dark oak wainscotting of the hallway and the tones of the markedly English voices, transported me into the atmosphere created by novels about British India. I was enchanted, even before I had cocktails which were served in a long narrow room at the left with a high mantled enormous fireplace facing the entrance. Sir Frederick was most interested to hear from me about the D'Oyly Carte Company, who were playing the Gilbert and Sullivan operas in New York when I left America. He wanted to know how his favorite English company was being received on Broadway. Of course I enthused, and should have liked the conversation to continue, but ultimately and always when a newly arrived American was present, the conversation turned to the all absorbing subject of the world-wide financial depression. We left soon afterwards.

Another English home where we attended a party later, belonged to Mr. Henry Morriss, who owns the NORTH CHINA DAILY NEWS, the leading British news organ in China, and who also owns the horse that won the then latest Derby. The latter fact was told me before the former, when I was introduced to him! His house was extremely Victorian in furnishings but not atmosphere. The party was given by Dr. Wu-Lien-Teh, Chinese Head of the Quarantine Service of the Nationalist Government, at Shanghai. Mr. Morriss, a friend of Dr. Teh had offered his house, as it was more spacious for a large party. Mr. Morriss, and Mr. Hallett Abend assisting, were mixing the cocktails themselves, because, they explained, the Chinese servants are not always careful about mixing the ingredients, and told of one experience in the past when the servants used gin instead of fruit juice to make up the necessary amounts of fluid called for in the receipt! There were many well-known people there, among them Mr. George Eumor-fopoulos, the Greek gentleman, who, in 1934, sold his collection of Chinese Art treasures to the British Museum, at a price that was said to be a gift, (I had met him previously at a reception of the Royal Asiatic Society, given for him and Sir Henry Burton of the British Museum). At this party I also met Sir Victor Sassoon, the one man I had read about, whom I had hoped to meet in Shanghai. Later at a luncheon, I was placed beside him and that experience was one of my big moments. He was fascinating and all I expected he might be, and I can well understand his reputation for captivating the ladies.

At my right at this same luncheon, was Mr. Arthur Bassette, the head of the British American Tobacco interests, who told me so much that was interesting that I could not resist telling him that he should write a book about his experiences. His answer was that he knew too much that could not be published, and if he wrote only what could be published his friends would laugh at him. I then told him that he must agree with my banker friend of thirty years experience in China who said, that when people were in China for a short time, they always wrote a book, but when they had been in China for a long time they were discouraged by the complexities of the task. Mr. B. agreed and added that most people made the mistake when they did write about China, of always trying to prove something, and usually became so obsessed with their own idea that they were blind to other equally important facts about Chinese life and psychology; that if they would only try to tell what they saw, stressing the point that they could only see any fact or question from their own point of view, one could believe more that is written about China, for it would take many minds, to see and understand the entire Chinese situation and nation. Then Sir Victor Sassoon, referring to a then recent article about him in an American magazine, added that one should be careful also to take all that was published about anyone or any institution in China, with a grain of salt! Well, anyway I should never be presumptuous enough with my meagre stay in China to try to prove anything anyway, and so I am trying to relate my experiences and others may draw their own conclusions. It is so easy to take an isolated occurrence to prove a preconceived idea about a race of people. One might say that all Chinese are superstitious because of the bronze lions in front of the British Hongkong Bank in Shanghai. Certain Chinese have rubbed and stroked the paws to a shining brightness, because they believed that they would become more courageous by so doing. But that does not prove that the Chinese as a race are any more superstitious than any other race, a statement often repeated by the journalist-lecturer critics of China.

The thought of British lions, and strength and power, reminds me of another famous man in Shanghai, Sir ____. As a boy he was a camel driver in Arabia and eventually became wealthy, and was knighted by the British King. He is a very old man now, short and stout, and lives with his bachelor son, Mother and I were invited to tea and to see his garden and famous house, entirely built of marble imported from Italy. Tea was served at a long table on the porch that extended the entire length of the house, about two hundred feet long, overlooking a wide lawn with a Chinese garden at the rear. A young violinist, recently arrived in Shanghai from a month's concert tour in

Japan, and his mother were the only other guests. Our host had offered him the use of his huge ballroom for his daily practice while in Shanghai, and I was wickedly amused by his efforts to be polite when a pet parrot, on a large perch a few feet from the table, screeched unmercifully at any rise in the conversation. It was explained that the parrot was very jealous, but no one suggested removing the bird to other quarters! While tea was being served, our host did most of the talking, telling us how irritated he was by the Chinese property owners adjoining his estate, who refused to sell their property at any reasonable price to him, because they knew that by holding out he would have to pay them more. Another proof that human nature is much the same in every country! A ten foot high marble wall completely surrounded his estate and only the tops of the neighboring dwellings were in sight. His house was three stories high, entirely of white marble, with white marble lions at each of the four corners of the roof. It was two hundred feet long and about half as wide, more like a museum than a private home. The glassed-in terrace where tea was served, was supported by large white marble columns that went up to the roof. Directly behind the tea table were tall grass doors which led into the ballroom of the house. This room was enormous with a ceiling three stories high, from which were hung glass chandeliers with four thousand bulbs, we were told. There was an electric motor used to raise and lower the chandeliers for cleaning, and they had a system of changing colored lights, like that in the Rainbow Room at Radio City. A staff of electricians, carpenters and plumbers are employed as regular household help, we were told. The Grand Lama of Thibet had been entertained here by our host for the Shanghai municipality at the request of Mayor Wu-Te-Chen. My mother and her husband had attended the party and told me about it. The Lama's sacred musicians played, and sat in the moonlight on the lawn just below the marble steps where we were. My mind was doing handsprings trying to realize that I was actually in the same house, a gorgeous mansion of white marble, where a Grand Lama had been entertained, talking to a man who had risen from being a camel driver in Arabia to a position where he could be knighted by the King of England. The rest of the house was very grand and filled with beautiful objects d'art and honorary gifts from British Indian Hebrew societies.

Our host discussed at length the great depression in America, and how it was beginning to affect Shanghai's prosperity as well, preventing him from giving big parties on account of criticism. I heard many other wealthy foreigners complaining in the same way and it was quite like home. One who was representing the interests of the Hardoon family was especially vehement. I was intrigued by tales about the Hardoons. Mr. Hardoon also an Arabian by birth, but now deceased, had married a Chinese woman who was a strict Buddhist. Her influence over him was so great, that all the Hardoon buildings in Shanghai, although modernistic in design, have a Buddha emblem on them somewhere. I noticed one block in particular, built in a half circle on a corner, with the emblems a few feet apart all around the top ledge of the building. I was told that when he died, as well as a Jewish funeral, his wife had the grandest possible Buddhist funeral too; that she later adopted twenty children who live with her in Shanghai! Certainly she cannot be lonely!

About a week before I left Shanghai Mother decided to try the dentist recommended to her by the aesthetic love cult dentist in Peking. I was terribly curious

about him and on inquiry found that he was ranked
as the tenth best dental surgeon in the world and had
credentials from the Mayos here in America; that his
father was a Spanish Count of great wealth; that he
had an independent income, and if he did not like you
he would not work for you; that he was an artist and
had one of the best collections of bronzes, Chinese
paintings and porcelains in Shanghai. His waiting
room was beautifully furnished with choice Chinese
antiques, paintings, furniture and rugs, but there was
no music as at the dentist's in Peking. His nephew,
a dark-eyed youth entertained us while we waited,
showing us some of the Doctor's artistic photography
taken in the interior of China. A few minutes later we
were ushered into the office, and he must have liked
us I thought, because he told his nephew to send away
the people in the waiting room for he would see no one
else that afternoon. He had a Chinese dentist assisting
him, talked incessantly, quoted poetry, discussed
porcelains and bronzes, invited us to his forthcoming
exhibition of art photography, while examining
mother's tooth. He exhibits in America and Europe
and we were told, was backed by Sir Victor Sassoon.
To me he was just one more unusual white man in the

Orient!

A few days later at lunch, my friend of thirty years experience in China, who had come to live at the Park Hotel for a time, asked if I would like to go to a Chinese play that evening. He said the plays started at five in the afternoon and lasted until after midnight, quite like O'Neill's "Strange Interlude", I thought. I accepted with alacrity but suggested that we go about eight-thirty as I felt that I never could sit through anything for that length of time! I did not know that you cannot reserve seats at a Chinese theatre but have to hire someone to sit in them until you arrive, so did not realize what I was asking. I had said that I wanted to go in a ricksha, so at eight-thirty we set forth in open rickshas. The theatre was in a Chinese section of the International Settlement about a mile from the Park Hotel and Bubbling Well Road. It was thrilling to go through the electric-lighted traffic of the Chinese streets at night, perched up high on the seat of the ricksha, that was gently joggled by the ricksha coolies, whose swaying back and bare pad-padding feet gave me the feeling that I was being bounced along on undulating rubber instead of a pavement. The misty haze, the twinkling lights and the red and gold business banners hanging out like flags from the stores, made everything mysteriously glamorous! We arrived at the theatre in a maze of ricksha and pedestrian traffic even at that late hour. It was on Foochow Road and was called Tien Tsan Wu Day, which I was told, means Toad Theatre. The outside was painted a bright Chinese red with all kinds of gold Chinese character banners hanging out on poles like flags from every possible ledge. The building was about three stories high and built on a perfect size of the average American theatre, and was painted again Chinese red with gold character-like designs. On the front of the balcony, bunches of roses were painted at intervals on a red background, a most gaudy effect. In front of each row of seats was a long narrow ledge and on this ledge in front of each person, were placed a dish of fruit, a dish of dried seeds, and on request a pot of hot tea, all included in the price of the ticket. I wondered how they drank the tea without cups, and was much amazed to see an elderly Chinese man next to me, take the tea pot in both hands and put the spout in his mouth, holding on the cover with his forefinger! All through the performance food vendors circulated through the aisles, selling food, anything from roast duck and fried duck skin to white, mushy-looking round cakes like doughnuts, only without any holes, speared through the middle, one on top of the other by a stick about eighteen inches long, and upright by the vendor. Periodically the ushers passed small baskets of hot, wet turkish towelling face cloths. One is supposed to wipe the face and hands and pass back the cloths to the ushers, who sling them one by one to other ushers in the rear, over the heads of the audience who sit beneath this barrage of flying wet cloths quite unperturbed. I did not use one myself, I need not add. I was amazed to see the accuracy with which they threw those cloths, never failing to reach the usher in the rear no matter how far they tossed them, sometimes a distance of thirty feet or more. I am purposely starting with a description of the audience and working in towards the stage, because the hub-bub and uproar among the spectators was so overpowering that it took me several minutes before I even noticed what was going on, on the stage. Everyone was chattering and talking, babies cried or slept in their mothers' arms, small children munched the food in front of them, and a general good time was had by all. Only occasionally one would see a Chinese watching the stage with rapt attention, but only for a few minutes at a time. From descriptions I had read of the Chinese theatre, my idea was very different. I had imagined self-contained property men, solemnly lifting furniture on and off the stage, with reserved and unhurried calm, making themselves as unobtrusive and lifeless as the properties they carried; actors who slowly took their positions and posed in a Charlie Chan calm, with hands tucked in sleeves, speaking their lines in the deep well modulated tones of the Chinese in our movie detective plays, and with no scenery as we know it; an audience of excessively silent, intellectual-looking people who would watch the play and might smile a knowing quiet smile occasionally during the performance, but otherwise would appear like living counterparts of the Stoics! Instead, I was overpowered by the din all around me and only by degrees could I wrench my attention from the audience, entirely Chinese except for ourselves, long enough to try to gather what was really going on on the stage. It was as large as our average American stage, but had an additional half circular platform extending out into the auditorium. The curtain came down at the back of this half circle, so that many scenes

were played in front of the curtain. At the left in front
of the curtain was the orchestra of about fifteen
Chinese pieces, cymbals, gongs, bells, a kind of wood
clapper and Chinese violins. At the stage right was a
constantly changing group of men and boy onlookers,
who came and went at will occasionally helping with
the properties and scenery. They were all very informal
and chatted away among themselves quite
unconcerned by the fact that they were on the stage,
and quite as conspicuous as the actors. A large red
carpet covered the whole stage, a very modern
departure my friend told me, in explanation of the
fact that one of the actors in a moment of stress forgot
the carpet and spat upon it! On the curtain, that did
not raise but pulled back like a portiere, there was
painted at one side a modern lady's slipper about
fifteen feet long, with Chinese characters beneath it
advertising shoes, and on the other side of the curtain
was painted an equally over-sized package of breakfast
food with corresponding Chinese characters
advertising that. The curtain was pulled back for the
really big scenes of the play, revealing scenery of the
old ten-twenty-thirty variety show in America, but
with superb lighting effects. In one scene a fire was

staged in a burning tower, with the hero on top fighting with the villain, and I was much perturbed wondering how they were going to rescue him! I was amazed to see an enormous hand with all the fingers, made I should think of papier-mache, in a dull gray, the arm part ribbed and collapsible like a paper lantern, stretch right out from the stage left and pick up the hero around the waist so that he dangled like a kitten held by the back of the neck! The most literal long arm of circumstance one could possibly imagine! I need not add that the villain was left to burn to death. After this grand scene I expected the audience to show some appropriate emotion; they took it all as a matter of course and went right on with their chatting and eating. The only times I saw more than a few taking notice, was when an actor's voice would rise to a shriller falsetto than usual, denoting approaching disaster of some sort, I supposed. Most of the actors spoke their lines in falsetto tones, and each actor seemed to have a musical motif which announced his arrival on the stage. As they were constantly going on and off, the din from the predominantly brassy Chinese instruments was terrific! The costumes were beautiful, colorful and magnificent, and the actors' use of hands, feet and facial expressions were superbly effective. They showed emotion through pantomime so well that the words even if I could have heard or understood them, were almost unnecessary. After about two hours, I had seen all I could stand for one evening. When we went outside it was pouring and there was nothing but a ricksha for conveyance. When you get into a ricksha with the rain top up, you cannot see out except through a narrow opening in the top part of the front rubber sheet, that hangs from a collapsible top like the top of a small buggy. When we arrived back at the hotel, my friend's face and collar were soaked. He had hung his head out over the top of the black rubber curtain of his ricksha, to keep my ricksha in sight all the way. I should have felt only gratitude for his good care of me, but could only think of how funny he must have looked with his face sticking out over the curtain of the ricksha! Anyway that rainy scary ride cured me of my longing for rickshas. All cooped up like that made me feel as helpless as I imagined a Chinese bride must feel. A bride is carried by coolies in a closed coach, with curtains drawn similar to a sedan chair. I had seen many wedding and funeral processions, the costumes of both the mourners and the wedding attendants are equally gorgeous, white for mourning and red for weddings predominating, and in sounds equally loud. One procession especially, I shall never forget, in the Chinese section not far from Bubbling Well Road. I heard a band, and as it drew nearer, the tune they were playing sounded strangely familiar. I could not really believe my ears when I recognized it as "A Bicycle Built For Two." I was even more amazed when a funeral procession with professional mourners and all the fixings, came into view! When I returned to the hotel, I asked my mother if I could really have heard right, and she told me that she had once heard a funeral band playing "Hail, Hail, The Gangs All Here;" that the Chinese bands pick up any foreign tune, not knowing the words of course, and adapt them to their needs. The words mean no more to them than would the words of a Chinese song to us, and since my return I have realized that most Americans understand the Chinese people about as well as they might understand the words of a Chinese song!

I left Shanghai on the S. S. Coolidge, the twenty-eighth of April. The usual stops of a number of hours were made at Kobe and Yokohoma, Japan. At Kobe, the harbor was the greatest possible contrast to the water front at Shanghai, Progressive prosperity permeates the atmosphere. I counted thirty big merchant ships at anchor and hundreds of small craft. All along the water front were cement warehouses, and many modern factories were visible in the distance; I might have thought I was landing at any American port, except for the faces and costumes of the Japanese people. My bargaining with the taxi drivers, (I say drivers, although I only talked with one, but there are always two, one drives and the other does the price setting), is a good example of the Japanese trading idea,

"How much to Motomachi St?" I asked.

"One yen," he answered.

"They tell me on boat, fifty sens to Mototomachi St." I answered.

"All right," he answered, as he saw other taxi drivers approaching although he was agreeing to take me for half what he originally asked. Sell at any price rather than allow the next fellow to get your customer!

Motomachi St. is a street of the old type with cobblestone pavements where automobiles are not allowed, and small one story buildings open to the street just as in the native shops in Shanghai. But here the stores were spotlessly clean, and where food was sold it was either under glass or in cellophane, such a contrast with Shanghai! In the afternoon I went to a department store, a cement block of modern design on the corner of a broad street paved with asphalt. Inside at the elevators, there were signs in English as well as Japanese, and the elevator girls wore khaki-colored dresses made like our girl scout uniforms, with little khaki overseas caps pinned literally over one ear! I wanted to buy a curling iron and went to the electric goods department on the fifth floor of this eight story building. On that same floor were the kitchen goods as well, and I had a sinking feeling when I looked at the complete line of tin and aluminum ware as well as everything electrical, and all so much cheaper than in America. For instance the electric curling iron I bought cost thirty-three cents American money, and the best invisible hairpins I have ever had, and double the usual amount, cost only three cents. The next day in Yokohoma, I saw many more of these department stores where I bought an all silk umbrella with a case for one dollar and seventy-five cents American money, and a cowhide, large size suit case with straps and locks for six dollars and eighty cents our money. When I was in Tokio, on my way to China, I inquired about the rates at the Imperial Hotel, which is the best hotel and modern in every detail, and found that one could stay there for three dollars and a half per day, American money, with all meals and service included. I should think that everyone who had a small independent income would settle in Tokio! The few hours in the afternoon before the ship sailed from Yokohoma, I spent in an Industrial Exposition which had opened two weeks before. It could compare with any of our expositions in size and variety of goods. I was astounded by the number of kinds of machines which are made in Japan, as well as all kinds of complicated looking parts for guns and battleships. There was a machine making cigarettes, and an exhibit of the whole process right through to putting them into packets. A young Japanese, in charge of the exhibit, seeing that I was a "foreigner" and alone, explained in perfect English, that the machines for making, and the cigarettes, were a government monopoly, "Cherry Cigarettes" they were called, and retailed for three cents for twenty, American money. I had a lot of fun wandering around the exhibition, after I became accustomed to being stared at as a curiosity, for I saw no other foreigners there. In a dark passage way, a crowd had collected to see a sort of side show. There were two separate stages with a partition, each about five feet in frontage and four feet in depth. The show was about to start on the first little stage and when the lights went on, I saw a life-sized figure of a Japanese man, and opposite him, a figure of a Japanese woman with a huge meat cleaver in her hands, and an enormous papier-mache peach on the floor between them, (symbol of longevity and fertility in China, but I did not know about Japan). A gong sounded, the mechanical figures became animated, the woman stood up, raised the battle axe cleaver and cracked it down on the peach. It opened in halves, and in the center was the animated figure of a naked little boy, who hopped and danced about excitedly. Then the lights went out in that stage, and there was a terrific banging on a drum at the next stage where the lights suddenly went on. I moved on with the crowd, and saw a wooded scene with primitive warriors dressed in animal skins, whacking at each other with big knotted wooden clubs. Then the lights went off and when they came on again the scene was

changed, modern buildings and parks were in the
background and were being bombarded by miniature
cannons, while anti-aircraft guns brought flaming
planes to earth, and all sorts of wonderful and awful
contraptions of modern warfare were in action! At
length it ended and the crowd moved on. Around the
corner there was a big display of a company which
made anti-aircraft guns. While we are preaching birth
control and peace, they are propagandizing for more
babies and armaments!

Further on I saw a poster I wanted, at a booth
where I found no one could speak English. I struggled
along for some time with motions, drawing more
and more curious attention to myself thereby, but
no one could understand me. Soon everyone in the
crowd was good naturedly trying to find out what
I wanted, until finally the humor of the situation
seemed to strike us all at the same time, and we all
began to laugh foolishly. Just then a young Japanese,
dressed in a uniform buttoned to the high-collared
neck, with a little round cap just like the German
military caps, came through the crowd and said in
stilted tones "You, English lady?" I almost shouted
"Yes, can you speak English?" because by that time I

had made up my mind I would get that poster if I had to climb up and take it down myself. He answered "I work hard, learn speak English!" After several efforts I was able to make him understand what I wanted, and he got the poster for me. I asked him if he was a guide, and he looked very insulted and said proudly, "I am student!" I thanked him and walked away, only to find that each time I stopped he was right at my elbow. I tried to ignore him but he stayed with me until I left the exposition, trying out his English on me and acting delighted each time I appeared to understand him. He finally said, "English very hard language, I can talk, you talk, I do not know you say." I discovered later from other people on the ship, that these students avail themselves of every opportunity to learn to speak English, following anyone who will talk to them. When I left him he asked for my address in the "States," and I wrote it out for him, then he tipped his cap and said, trying out a language book love-taking formula, "Farewell, I wish you happy journey!" I carried away with me that look on his face of expectancy, watching to see if his English took that time. I went back to the ship with a feeling mixed with foreboding, for I felt that competition from this nation of "go-getters," is something to fear.

On the ship I heard the usual gushy stories from middle-aged ladies about "darling little Japanese guides I had, and you know he sent me flowers when I left" and about "the lovely little Japanese women in their pretty kimonos," but very little enthusiasm for their very apparent efficiency and modernity. If mentioned these qualities were condoned as "spoiling the old Japan." It reminded me of a remark of a prominent negro in the States who said that there is no dangerous resentment against the negroes in the United States, as long as they continue to be servants, comedians or musicians, in other words made to feel that they are an inferior race, only capable of certain activities in modern society. I feel that this is the same attitude that the average Anglo-Saxon takes towards both the Chinese and the Japanese. As long as they offer no marked competition in the industrial or financial world they will be tolerated and even liked! But of course, I am only speaking of my own reactions to the contacts I happened to make during my short stay in the Orient.

One evening a few days out from Yokohama, a gentleman remarked that we had all been in the

Orient for the past six weeks and when we returned, the people back home would ask us what our solution would be of the problems of the far East, and, from what we had seen, what our predictions would be about the future relations between China and Japan. He was right; everyone I have met has naïvely asked that very question. Although I was only there six weeks, I was very fortunate in being able to meet, due to Dr. Cleveland's position in the Nationalist Government, many people who have lived in China and have studied the Oriental problem for years. My belief is that China will probably be dominated by Japan for a number of years, but eventually will absorb beneficially to herself, the invaders, as she has periodically done for thousands of years. One has the feeling that whatever might happen in one generation is really of no moment, for the span of life is merely an incident in the vast plan of race survival. With this idea in mind I was almost shocked when a nice gentleman told me that he was quite upset by an opinion of a guide in Japan, but added that of course he was only a guide, who told him that Christianity in Japan was making no progress at all! I realized then that my mental processes had strayed far from their

New England entourage, because at that moment it seemed to me that it did not make much difference whether Christianity succeeded in the Orient or not! As a matter of fact the success of the Christian idea is greatly hampered by the thought that Christianity is so closely linked with the ideas of commerce in the minds of the Chinese people, that they are apt to blame the Christian religion for the misdeeds of all white foreigners. Just before I left Shanghai, there was a lot of bad feeling about the American silver clause decision, as it was asserted that a great many small Chinese shop keepers were being ruined and the Americans were being blamed for it. Questions of values of silver and gold and commodity prices are quite beyond my comprehension, but I do think of silver as a mineral that one would not pile up in back alleys like kindling, and that is what I saw in the alleyway beside the Hongkong Bank on the Bund. Silver bars were actually piled up there, and coolies were carrying the bars in wheelbarrows, and dumping them out like logs of wood. This sounds like a fairy tale but so did a great deal of what I saw and heard in China. After six weeks in Shanghai there were few tales I would reject without investigation, and recent events strengthen my feeling that anything may happen in China. It is cleaner and safer and more comfortable to live in the United States, of course; nevertheless, I feel like the young aviator returning from Siam, I met on the S. S. Coolidge, who said, "It's grand to be back home, but I hope I shall be sent back to the Orient."

SHANGHAI: 1935

About The Authors

Ruth Day (1892-1964) was born in Boston as Ruth Van Buren Hugo, and in 1915 married Morgan Glover Day, a member of a prominent family from Springfield, Massachusetts. They settled in Springfield where they raised two sons. In 1935, she traveled to Shanghai to visit her mother Jane, who was then married to Dr. Frederick A. Cleveland (1865-1946), who was then in China to assist the National Government with its financial administration.

Andrew David Field is a scholar of Chinese and East Asian history. He has published several books and articles on the history of Shanghai. He currently lives in Shanghai with his wife Mengxi and their two daughters, Sarah and Hannah. He is a professor and administrator at Duke Kunshan University.

9 789888 552610